Tijuana:
Urbanization in a Border Culture

Tijuana:

Urbanization in a Border Culture

by
John A. Price

UNIVERSITY OF NOTRE DAME PRESS
NOTRE DAME   LONDON

Library of Congress Cataloging in Publication Data

Price, John A   1933-
    Tijuana: urbanization in a border culture. *see slip*

    Bibliography: p. 187 - 191.
    1. Urbanization—Baja California (State) 2. Tijuana, Mexico
(Baja California) 3. Mexico—Foreign relations—United States.
4. United States—Foreign relations—Mexico. I. Title.
HN120.B3P75   301.36'1'09722   72-12641
ISBN 0-268-00477-3
ISBN 0-268-00495-1 (pbk.)

Printed in the United States of America by
NAPCO Graphic Arts, Inc., New Berlin, Wisconsin

iv

This study was produced through the U.S.-Mexico Border Studies Project at the University of Notre Dame, under the direction of Julian Samora, sponsored by a grant from the Ford Foundation. The opinions expressed in the report do not necessarily represent the views of the Foundation.

Contents

Foreword

This is the fourth book to be published under the auspices of U.S.-Mexico Border Studies Project of the University of Notre Dame.

This project was begun in 1968 with a grant from the Ford Foundation. The objective of the grant was to come to a better understanding of Mexican-Americans in the United States through research endeavors and publications.

The three earlier books were Dr. Ernesto Galarza's *Barrio Boy* and *Spiders in the House and Workers in the Field* and Professor Julian Samora's *Los Mojados: The Wetback Story*.

In this book Professor Price takes a look at the phenomenon of urbanization in a border city, in this instance Tijuana.

The northern border of Mexico is one of the fastest-growing areas in the world, and the populations tend to settle in a few urban centers. This great population movement from other parts of Mexico has a profound effect on the border region on both sides of the imaginary political line. There is no place in the world where a phenomenon of this magnitude is taking place. What happens in the border region has ramifications and implications throughout the United States and Mexico.

Professor Price and his students have looked at this

phenomenon of urbanization on the Mexican border and have attempted to give us an understanding of the dynamics of the situation as it involves two nation states.

We hope that this first study of urbanization in the border region will lead to further research of a more complex situation which in turn might provide data which both nations might use in their consideration of the immense problems evident in the region.

Julian Samora

University of Notre Dame
March, 1973

Preface

This is a book about the processes of urban development as they are influenced by the context of Mexican border culture. The central thesis is that the nature of a city is best explained in cultural dynamics that are broader than the city itself: geographical, historical, demographic, economic, political. Ethnographic portraits or community studies that focus simply on the city itself are necessary to describe the character of the city, but they are just the beginning in the understanding of why the city developed the way it did and the ability to make predictions about the city's future.

I began by doing descriptive community studies of Tijuana and the neighboring border city of Tecate. However, in order to understand this raw data it soon became clear that I needed to know about such things as the geography and history of the region and many other lines of significant influence that led away from the study of these as isolated cities. A survey of cities along the northern border of Mexico then indicated so many similarities and parallel sequences of development that a general Mexican border culture was hypothesized. This finally led to an examination of the unique features of border cultures themselves.

This book, then, is as much about the contexts of

Tijuana as the city itself because, I maintain, we can best understand its important dynamics only through those contexts. I begin with chapters on urbanization in northern Mexico (Chapter 1) and in the state of Baja California (Chapter 2). Two chapters describe Tijuana in terms of history (Chapter 3) and contemporary life (Chapter 4). Two chapters focus on the social segments of smuggling (Chapter 5) and prison life (Chapter 6) as explorations into some of the special problems of Tijuana. Chapter 7 steps back to compare Tijuana as a tourist-oriented border city with the neighboring industrially oriented border city of Tecate. The last three chapters are brief theoretical discussions. Chapter 8 analyzes Tijuana's frontier setting and its history of cultural adaptations. Chapter 9 examines three topics in the ethnology of international border cultures: boundary marking, screening, and smuggling. Finally, Chapter 9 concludes with an analysis of international symbiosis in relation to Tijuana.

Northern Mexico is a distinct region of Mexico that has been influenced by the United States, but it is still basically Mexican in culture. In fact, the differences between the cultures on the U.S. and Mexican sides of the border are extreme, some of the greatest differences between any two adjoining societies in the world. On the U.S. side is an affluent, highly industrialized society that is English in language, British in legal traditions, and slow in population growth. On the other side is a slowly industrializing society that is Spanish in language, Roman in legal traditions, and rapid in population growth. Anglo and Latin cultures come face-to-face at this border.

Border cities everywhere become economically caught up in the reciprocal marketing of goods and services which are higher priced or illegal in one of the countries. Thus the first boom to the Mexican border towns came during the American crusade that brought on Prohibition and outlawed gambling. During World War II the Mexican border towns supplied many items that were rationed or simply in short supply in the U.S. Now, although illegal in Mexico as well, Mexico has adjusted to a new market demand and supplies Americans with some 300 tons of marijuana each year. However, illegal commerce directly touches the lives of very few Mexicans and for decades now the border cities have increasingly become industrial and commercial centers. Vice is no longer at all characteristic of the border towns.

Although we still see a few squatter villages and a moderate unemployment rate, northern Mexico has among the highest wages in Latin America. These high wages have attracted a great many migrants from central Mexico, making northern Mexico the country's fastest-growing area, about 5 percent per year. Tijuana had grown to a city of 335,125 people by the 1970 census.

New arrivals from the interior typically come first to Tijuana's Zona Norte, where there are cheap hotels, country-style bars with wandering *mariachi* bands, the older style open markets, and a squatter village in the riverbed next to the highway. Moving up the social scale somewhat, people then typically build their own homes in the newer and more outlying districts of the city. Some of these lower-class housing areas began as squatter settlements and evolved into privately owned *colonias.* The *fraccionamiento*, or subdivision, is a new kind of housing alternative for middle-class Mexicans. These developments, although providing rather small houses, do have paved streets, running water, and sewer systems. The older upper class tend to live either on ranches or in homes with high walls close to the downtown center, while the newer upper class have begun to move out to the hills surrounding the city.

The preceding description should demonstrate the inaccuracy of the tourist stereotype of the Mexican border city as a center of vice and poverty. The initial perception of Tijuana as an ugly city of slums that is acquired by American visitors simply does not correspond with the Tijuanese view of their city. There is a personal perspective or reason for looking deeper than the usual tourist into border cultures. There is satisfaction in understanding the way cultures work and the problems and aspirations of foreign neighbors. To most visitors to the border areas this personal perspective is sufficient. They enjoy the exploration of a different culture with its distinctive foods, dress, arts. A few discover that the most satisfying way to be a tourist is to explore actively the country and its culture rather than passively joining the crowds in the commercial tourist districts. Church services, amateur bullfights, local rodeos, informal conversations in the plaza, and visiting in local homes are often more enjoyable than staying in resort motels or souvenir shopping.

People who retain a long-term interest in a border culture occasionally go on to historical or ethnographic descriptions or become involved in applied work to solve local problems. The applied work is particularly important because the border cultures that develop usually contain many stresses as a direct result of their border location and border-screening processes. National governments are often unable to solve these problems because of the extensive international cooperation that would be called for and because of the difficulties inherent in screening, national defense, international legal jurisdictions, and so on. Thus individuals and associations who work informally in both countries to solve local problems perform services that are difficult for governments to perform.

Acknowledgments

While at the University of California, Los Angeles, and San Diego State College between 1967 and 1970 I directed ethnographic field courses in Tecate and Tijuana and seminars on such phenomena as immigration, smuggling, and urbanization in northern Mexico. Over two dozen students in these courses worked with me on research in the Tijuana area. Research on urbanization in northern Mexico in 1969 and work on smuggling in 1970 was supported by grants from the U.S. Mexico Border Studies Project of the University of Notre Dame, Julian Samora, Director. Among the several Mexican scholars who have helped me, Victor Peñalosa of Tecate is preeminent.

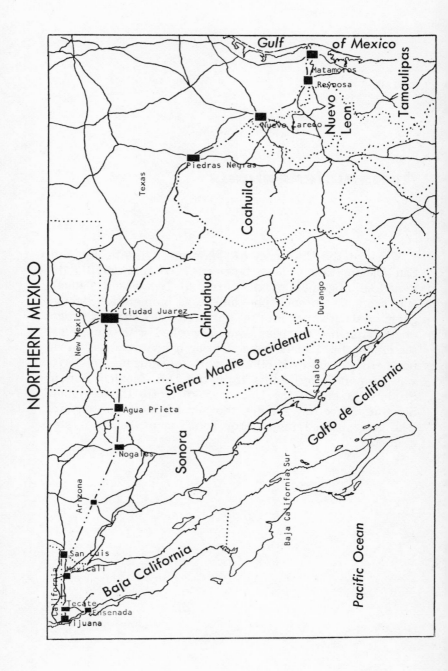

i: *The Urbanization of Northern Mexico*

Growth of a Frontier

Within the vast, generally arid, lands of Southwestern U.S. and northern Mexico important new cultures are undergoing a florescent, creative growth. While these cultures have historical antecedents that go back for centuries, they are now essentially urban and of the twentieth century. Prehistorically and in its early Spanish history the high cultural center was central Mexico. Agriculture, weaving, pottery, and many other traits diffused into the Indian cultures of this region from the south. It was the "outback," the far periphery of a higher civilization, aboriginally and in all of its early history. Now, in less than a century of explosive growth, it is the home of vital urban-industrial cultures.

While the American and Mexican cultures of this region are very different, the facts of their similar land and climate and their frontier location led to parallel adaptations. Beginning with an early cattle and sheep pastoralism, agrarian industry has flourished recently with concentrated irrigation agriculture, particularly of such warm-weather crops as cotton and citrus fruits. Mining and petroleum extraction are major industries on both sides of the international border. The fact that irrigated agriculture is so concentrated here has led to an intensive use of a small amount of the total land and a high concentration of people in cities. Thus, although aridity of the area has led to a low total population density, the proportion of people who live in cities is high.

The historical background of this area is marked by the long survival of desert-adapted Indian cultures, relative isolation from centers of civilization in central Mexico and the eastern U.S., and a classical kind of frontier with substantially free land in an area where there is a low population density. Frontier cultures stressed rugged individualism and self-sufficiency, achievement over ascription, opportunities as well as hardships, freedom from legal constraints, and a blunting of fine arts, literature, and the social niceties. Mexicans talk about Baja California, for example, in much the same way that Americans and Canadians talk about Alaska and the Northern Territories. This frontier background has contributed a distinctive character even to the developing urban cultures of the area. The traditional ascriptive social classes are almost meaningless in the North because of the strength of egalitarianism. Also it seems that the separation of the people of northern Mexico from the historical heartland of Mexican culture and the ever-present contrasts that Mexican culture has with American culture makes these northern Mexicans more conscious of their Mexican heritage and more patriotic about it than in Mexico generally.

Another factor in the uniqueness of the area is that two quite different cultural traditions and ethnic populations meet and intermingle here. This has continued to be a frontier area in the sense of the interpenetration of U.S. and Mexican societies. In the middle 1800's this area was the scene of the U.S.-Mexican War that helped to determine the current international boundary. The arid land, low population density, and unexplored and unsettled character of the country led to its acceptance as the international border zone. It had been a buffer zone between the Spaniards and the English, Russians, and French, and it became a transitional zone between U.S. and Mexican cultures. It was an important staging area for the Mexican Revolution in 1910, and it has continued to exert pressures for democracy in Mexico. The north has been the source of such revolutionaries as Francisco I. Madero, Pancho Villa, Venustiano Carranza, and Alvaro Obregon.

This chapter focuses primarily on the six states of northern Mexico: Baja California, Sonora, Chihuahua, Coahuila, Nuevo Leon, and Tamaulipas. These states form a regional grouping for several reasons. Principal among these are their aridity, their similar historical backgrounds, their communication with the U.S., and their recent urbanization.

The industrialization of the U.S. brought railways, industries, and irrigation projects into several parts of the northern states. Ensenada was started through foreign land-and-mining promotion, and Mexicali began when Americans developed an irrigation project with water from the Colorado River. Monterrey and Saltillo developed into commercial centers for mining and stock raising that was primarily stimulated by foreign interests.

This northern region contains 41 percent of the nation's land area, but in 1970 it contained only 17 percent of the nation's population. About one-half of the land is desert or near desert, and almost all of the agricultural potential that can exist without irrigation has been in use for a long time. In line with its aridity it had a population density of only 11 inhabitants per square kilometer in 1970. However, the agrarian population of the region tends to be concentrated in the areas where irrigated agriculture can be carried out. The Mexicali Valley has long been irrigated, and now about one-half million acres of irrigated land have been recently added to both the Lower Rio Grande and the Rio Fuerte Basin in Sonora. Also, the growing importance in the northern border states of manufacturing, commerce, and foreign tourism has led to a high urban concentration of people in the region. In fact, in terms of the proportion of the population who live in cities *the northern border is the most urban region in Mexico.* While the national urban proportion shifted from 51 percent to 60 percent between 1960 and 1970, the urban proportion of the northern border states shifted in the same years from 64 percent to 85 percent. The growth of industry has also contributed to a great migratory influx of people from other parts of Mexico, so that *the northern border has had the highest population growth rate of any major region in Mexico since 1940,* around 45 percent per decade (Secretaria de Industria de Comercio, 1967; Whetten, 1968).

We get some perspective of how great this growth is when we realize that Latin America generally has the highest population growth rate of any continental-size area in the world and that Mexico has one of the highest growth rates in Latin America. Thus, with an average annual growth rate that is now near 5 percent *northern Mexico is one of the fastest growing regions in the world today.* Three demographic changes in Mexico coincide to produce this phenomenon: a high natural increase of births over deaths, a rural to urban shift, and a general migration northward for higher wages. These demographic changes are producing vast cultural changes and some social problems. Perhaps the most surprising thing of all is that such extensive cultural change is taking place with so little cultural stress and social disintegration.

Mexican Demography

The growth and urbanization of the northern border states is taking place as an integral part of a general population boom and urbanization in Mexico. The high birth rate of about 43 births per 1,000 inhabitants has been maintained while improved diet and medical practices have caused the death rate to fall dramatically from

26.6 per 1,000 inhabitants in 1930 to only 9.9 per 1,000 inhabitants in 1970 (United Nations, 1972). Life expectancy at birth rose from about 33 years in 1930 to 61 years for males and 64 years for females in 1970. The combination of a stable high birth rate and a declining death rate resulted in an accelerating rise in the rate of natural increase of the population from 1.7 percent per year in 1930 to the extremely high rate of 3.5 percent in 1970. The latter is one of the highest rates of increase in the world, and Mexico's population is now increasing by about one and one-half million persons per year. The mean rate of annual growth of the world's population is about 2.0 percent (U.S. Bureau of Census, 1972).

While Asia, Africa, and Latin America generally have barely been able to maintain their prewar per capita food production, Mexico has doubled its per capita production of staple foods (Freithaler, 1968). Mexico's food production has increased at a significantly greater rate than its population growth, thus allowing for a declining proportion of the population to do the farming while others migrate to the cities for jobs in manufacturing and commerce. Irrigation projects brought new land into use, improved seeds were used, and agricultural information services were provided by the government. Since the people are being fed, Mexico tends to look at its population increase in positive, nationalistic terms. A large population thus means national prominence and a significant population base for undertaking industrialization and other programs of national development.

The general statistical comparison between the U.S. and Mexico seen in Table 1 will provide a perspective on Mexican demography (Ruddle and Hamour, 1972; United Nations, 1972; U.S. Bureau of Census, 1972). It can be noted that *Mexico now has a higher population density than the U.S.*, as the high birth rate of Mexico has its effects. We find that the expenditure of gross national product is more in government hands in the U.S. than in Mexico. Mexico relies on a high consumption of cereals

TABLE 1

Comparisons Between the U.S. and Mexico

	U.S.	Mexico
Population per square mile	57	65
Crude birth rate, per 1,000	18.2	43.4
Government expenditure of GNP	21%	6%
Daily per capita food consumption		
Calories	3,290	2,620
Cereals, gms.	145	305
Meat, gms.	243	44
Distribution per 100 population		
Motor vehicles	52	4
Telephones	59	3
Radio receivers	143	26
Television receivers	39	5
Housing		
Average persons per room	.7	2.9
Piped water (potable)	94%	49%
Proportion of the economically active population engaged in manufacturing	23%	10%

such as corn, while the U.S. has a high consumption of meat. The U.S. also has a higher per capita ownership of motor vehicles, communication facilities, and housing facilities. The proportion of the economically active population engaged in manufacturing is a rough index of industrialization, although the U.S. can be considered as moving into a postindustrial stage that draws more people into the sector of services than into manufacturing. These indices, both as statements of absolute conditions and as comparisons between two neighboring countries, help us appreciate the material bases involved in the Mexican migration to the northern border states as part of a larger northern migration that cannot be understood fully without reference to the attraction of the affluence of the United States. The United States receives as immigrants numbers equal to about 2 percent of Mexico's total annual population increase, but it is a massive stimulant in several indirect ways to the development of northern Mexico.

An important feature of Mexican demography is the primacy of Mexico City, a city with just over 3 million people (Ruddle and Hamour, 1971). Mexico City has traditionally had the status of a primate city. It was the major urban center under the Aztecs and under the Spaniards. Under the republic it has remained the seat of the federal government, the center of the nation's commerce and industry, and the major location for institutions of the church, higher learning, and the arts. It became the focal point for the nation's commercial, educational, and artistic investments and an attraction for its most talented people, so that the capability for an efficient industrial capacity was developed. About two-thirds of the nation's professional education facilities are in Mexico City. And about two-thirds of the foreigners who live in Mexico reside in Mexico City, although since 1900 the foreign population of Mexico has always been less than 1 percent of the total population. In line with this concentration of resources Mexico City has had a consistently high growth rate.

In 1940 there were only four cities in Mexico with a population of more than 100,000, and now there are about thirty such cities. In the north this growth has been marked by Monterrey as an industrial center, Chihuahua as a mining center, Mexicali as an agricultural center, and C. Juarez and Tijuana as centers of border commerce. To the individual it may simply mean that he cannot get a job in Mexico City at a wage that will provide a satisfying life for his family, while he can get what to him is a decent wage elsewhere, particularly now in the northern border states. With high population growth and urban migration rates both areas have unemployment rates that would be considered high by industrialized countries, but many new job opportunities are now available in the north.

Northern Mexico

The region of the northern border states has consistently had the highest growth rate of any region in the nation since 1940. Growth within the individual states of the region has been uneven, with Baja California consistently having the highest growth rate in the last 30 years, and Coahuila the lowest. All the states now have a population of over 1 million.

Geographically there are two major divisions of the north: an east-west split due to the Sierra Occidental and a north-south gradiation related to proximity to and influence from the United States. As a result, the north is not well integrated as a region. Because of the north-south trend of the mountains and the southern location of Mexico City, the highways and railroads of the north have a north-south trend. The greatest division within the north is between Baja California and Sonora to the west and the other states to the east. For example, Nogales is only 375 miles by air route from C. Juarez, but in order to drive between the two cities on Mexican soil one must travel 1,611 miles, south and then northwest to skirt the massive mountain chain of the Sierra Occidental. A railroad (nine years to complete, including 39 bridges and 76 tunnels) has finally been built across the mountains from Chihuahua to Topolabampo, but there are as yet no highways to directly link the north. Mexico lost the only reasonable place to cross this mountain chain in its northern territory when it sold the Gadsden Purchase to the United States in 1853.

One of the results of this lack of integration is that the northern immigration is divided into western and eastern streams. Thus immigrants to Tijuana, for example, come primarily from Mexico's western states. This geographical division of the north may also determine to a considerable degree whether an immigrant to the United States goes to California (the recipient of about 50 percent of the annual Mexican immigration to the U.S.) or Texas (the recipient of about 23 percent of the annual Mexican immigration to the U.S.).

A feature of cultural geography that is relevant to the north is the attraction of higher incomes in the border cities. The nine major border municipalities have per capita incomes that range up to over three times the national average. Still, there are important differences between these municipalities. Cities with high average incomes such as Tijuana, Mexicali, and C. Juarez more than doubled their populations in the 1950s, while cities with relatively low average incomes such as Piedras Negras and Matamoros increased 45 percent and 39 percent respectively (Programa National Fronterizo, 1961).

About one-fifth to one-third of the wages earned by residents of these cities are earned in the United States, an indication of their economic dependence. Additionally, the border municipalities collectively take in about 70 percent of the money spent by foreign tourists in Mexico, which totals about $1.5 billion each year. In several of these cities international trade, beyond commuting Mexicans and American tourists, is a major basis for employment and a strong link to the United States. The major border municipalities have more commerce with the U.S. (9.6 billion pesos in 1960) than they have with the Mexican interior (5.0 billion pesos). The trade balance with the U.S. is unfavorable, but it is offset by receipts from Mexican workers in the U.S. and the expenditures of U.S. tourists. The trade balance is unfavorable because the northern border area has insufficient exportable products and, due to the long distance to the concentration of industry in central Mexico, insufficient domestic merchandise.

Northern Cities

Tijuana developed out of a ranching center to become a city officially in 1890. The American Prohibition and U.S. reforms against such activities as gambling, prostitution, and boxing spurred the development of Mexican towns all along the border, but Tijuana was the closest Mexican town for the large population of Southern California, so Tijuana developed into Mexico's major center of tourism. Mexicali began in 1901 when water first flowed through an American-built irrigation system that ran a canal on the Mexican side. In the early 1900s American firms controlled the agriculture in the Mexicali Valley, but they were gradually replaced by the Mexican Revolution's establishment of *ejidos*, or "public-land" cooperatives, throughout the Valley. The city developed into a large commercial center for the agriculturalists of the Mexicali Valley. Nogales, the next city to the east, is on the shortest route from interior Mexico to Tucson and Phoenix. It is a railhead and trucking center with a moderate number of tourists coming down from Arizona.

Paso del Norte was selected as a mission site in 1659, a military post was established, and by 1749 the El Paso-Juarez Valley had six missions and a population of 3,045 (Valencia, 1968). Paso del Norte was a small farming and way-station community on the route between Chihuahua and Santa Fe for over two centuries. It was named Ciudad Juarez in 1888. By 1930 the municipality of Juarez had a population of 43,138, two cottonseed oil mills, two soap factories, a nail factory, and six cotton gins, although tourism had become its major industry. Like most of the border cities, Juarez began an explosive growth after 1940, but unlike the other cities, Juarez had a large city in El Paso immediately across the border on the U.S. side of the Rio Grande. Thus Juarez is unique among the border cities in being extremely closely integrated with a major American metropolis. One indication of the high degree of integration of these two cities is the existence since 1889 of a streetcar line between the cities. Today this line carries over 6.5 million passengers a year. A controversial fact of the integration is that thousands of people work illegally in El Paso.

In 1900 El Paso on the U.S. side had a population of 15,096, almost double that of Juarez at the time. El Paso developed the smelting of ores, oil refining, the manufacture of cement, and cotton milling. By 1970 El Paso had grown to 322,000, but had been surpassed in the 1960's in population by Juarez, which reached 436,054 in 1970. The physical aspects of the two cities are very different. Juarez has a much higher population density with a heavy and almost continuous concentration of settlement. El Paso is scattered out in loose settlements of suburbs as satellites around the downtown area. Juarez has an exclusively gridiron pattern of streets, while in El Paso the streets tend to follow the natural contours of the hills. Juarez historically was centered in the Latin American style of a plaza, church, and government offices, but the center has been essentially lost in the unplanned growth of the city. El Paso is growing along lines set down in a 1925 master city plan, while Juarez moves from one piecemeal improvization to the next and is lacking in such fundamentals for modern city planning as comprehensive zoning controls.

Piedras Negras, Nuevo Laredo, Reynosa, and Matamoros all lie along the Rio Grande across from southern Texas, an area with the lowest income level along the border. This is an irrigated agricultural valley, so these cities are commercial centers for the processing and shipping of agricultural products. In addition, Reynosa is the oil-refining center for northwest Mexico. Matamoros is potentially a seaport. Although it has access to the sea, Matamoros and a large surrounding district relies on Brownsville, Texas, for exporting its cotton and ores. The per capita income of Matamoros in 1960 ($401) was almost 50 percent above the national average, but it was still the lowest average income of the major border communities (Dillman, 1968). The growth of these cities that border southern Texas is much slower than the other border cities.

There are several major cities in the north that are not at the border. Monterrey, a city of 830,836 in 1970, is the nation's leading industrial center after Mexico City. It has the largest iron-and-steel works in the country, and it manufactures such things as chemicals, glass, and textiles. The Gulf and northeast area are Mexico's major sources of the fossil fuels coal and oil, so crucial for industrialization. Torreon, Chihuahua, and Hermosillo are commercial centers for mining, cattle ranching, and some forestry and agriculture. Saltillo is famous for its bright woolen cloth and its silverwork.

The Southwest U.S.

The Southwest United States has been a strong stimulant for the growth of northern Mexico. Initially U.S. capital and entrepreneurship was directly involved in the development of mining, irrigation agriculture, the petroleum industry, and the tourist industry in northern Mexico. For example, the breweries, racetracks, and casinos in the booming Mexican towns of the 1920s were predominantly owned and operated by U.S. citizens.

The Mexican Revolution and Mexican nationalism have since removed most of the direct U.S. investment and operation of companies in Mexico. Mexico uses little foreign capital and rejects the offers of such international development programs as the U.S. Peace Corps. The recent U.S. stimulus of growth in northern Mexico is primarily indirect, in such forms as international trade, the export of industrial technology, tourism, and the employment of Mexicans in the U.S.

About three-fourths of Mexico's trade is with the U.S. The U.S. particularly receives metals, cotton, coffee, cattle, vegetables, henequen, and sugar in return for manufactured items, machinery, railroad equipment, and motor vehicles. Mexico generally runs a deficit in this trade, but balances its books through U.S. tourist expenditures, other border transactions, and remittances from Mexican workers in the U.S. In 1965 Mexican income was $278 million from foreign tourists (Mexican tourists abroad spent $119 million), and $12 million from remittances by Mexican laborers in the U.S. (Banco Nacional de Comercio Exterior, 1966). One recent significant type of return of U.S. business to the Mexican border area is the establishment of dual plant operations under Mexico's Border Industrialization Program with the labor-intensive assembly plant in Mexico and certain freedoms of import and export. The approximately 150 factories that had been established by mid-1969 in Mexico under this program represent a capital investment of some $30 million and the employment of about 18,000 Mexican workers. U.S. labor organizations have complained that the Mexican program depresses wages along the U.S. side of the border. However, the U.S. Chamber of Commerce claims that this program is diverting industrial assembly that the U.S. would otherwise carry out in Asia, not in the U.S., and that an estimated 80 percent of every dollar spent on wages in Mexico's border plants returns to the U.S. in wholesale and retail purchases.

Strong differences between the states have developed with much higher population densities in California and Texas, a high growth rate in California and Arizona, and the high income and education level of California. New Mexico has no significant impact on border dynamics. Very few Mexicans migrate to New Mexico, and there are no major border-crossing points between New Mexico and Mexico. The Spanish-speaking people who do live in New Mexico are primarily descendants of the early Spanish settlers, so that in 1960 over 96 percent of them were born in the United States (Samora, 1966; U.S. Bureau of Census, 1972).

Chicago, Detroit, and other northern U.S. cities have attracted significant numbers of Mexican immigrants since about 1920, but the majority of the U.S. Spanish-speaking population still resides in the Southwest. Los Angeles, the San Francisco Bay area, El Paso, and San Antonio have the major urban concentrations of Spanish-speaking peoples, but they are also scattered in hundreds of other cities and towns of the Southwest. Mexican-Americans in Texas constitute about 10 percent of the total work force (Texas A. & M. University, 1966). The immediate border zone has a high Spanish-speaking population, so that Spanish is the predominant language of San Ysidro and Calexico in California, Nogales in Arizona, and several border cities in Texas. These border cities typically accept Mexican currency in retail shops without question. They are also really *dual cities* with the largest part in Mexico, a smaller part in the United States, and both usually with a predominantly Spanish-speaking population.

For example, the dual city of San Luis, Arizona—San Luis Rio Colorado, Sonora, has a population of 50,000 in the municipio on the Mexican side and 2,000 on the U.S. side. The U.S. town looks like a new American shopping center with cement curbs and gutters, wide sidewalks, and large glass-front stores. However, the American town is primarily Mexican-American with Spanish signs, Mexican currency in common use, and about 75 percent of the license plates on the cars along the main streets are Mexican. San Luis Rio Colorado is a commercial center for a cotton-growing region, but it buys much of its consumer goods in San Luis, Arizona, while at the same time people in the Yuma, Arizona, area find it convenient to buy Mexican goods in San Luis Rio Colorado. In another case, the cattle town of Agua Prieta, Sonora, is highly dependent on Douglas, Arizona, for its consumer goods and some wage-earning, while the Mexican city offers about a dozen tourist shops for the people in southeast Arizona. It is believed that this dependence will decrease when the paved highway is completed to link Agua Prieta to interior Mexico.

Despite the strong symbiotic relations between dual cities—dissimilar, yet mutually beneficial to one another— the coalescence of their Anglo and Hispanic populations is quite small. While there are word borrowings between languages, for example, and some individuals speak both languages, there is a strong persistence of two mutually exclusive societies, each speaking its own language. The Spanish-speaking population is particularly large, vital, and insulated from the English-speaking population along the U.S. side in the Rio Grande River basin. In some of these border areas the Spanish-speaking population makes up from 50 percent to 85 percent of the total population. There seems to be a critical self-supporting level for effective ethnicity in terms of population size, of a few thousand, in which the people of neighborhoods, schools, and industries are predominantly Spanish-speaking. The full complement of social institutions has some Spanish-speaking staff. There may still be thousands of Anglos in the local population, but they insulate themselves from significant personal contact with the Spanish-speaking population, while at the same time the Spanish-speaking population protects itself by excluding the Anglos. Rubel (1966) said the Anglos of Texas "studiously ignore" the Latin Americans of Texas. While business as usual goes on between the populations, there is a mutual conspiracy of silence on significant personal levels, and neither society knows much about the other.

Social Dynamics of the Border

The separatism discussed above is marked in the cultures on the U.S. and Mexican sides of the border. D'Antonio and Form (1965) wrote that the Anglos of El Paso "just don't know many of the cultured people of Juarez, who in many cases are more cultured than they are." Their contacts with Mexicans are primarily with wetback maids, gardeners, and braceros. The same writers also found that Juarez was politically more monolithic and centrally controlled than El Paso. They write that the Juarez elite are usually educated in the U.S., can speak English well, are knowledgeable about Mexican-U.S. linkages, and are often forced into a subordinate position of deference when dealing with the more ethnocentric El Paso influentials. In disaster relief along the border Ellwyn Stoddard found that U.S. relief goods were presented in such a manner as to threaten the *dignidad* of the Mexican representatives and were therefore habitually refused. The border zone is culturally transitional between American and Mexican societies, but the transition occurs primarily among Mexican-Americans who live on the U.S. side and who acculturate to American society.

Anglo-Americans rarely migrate or acculturate to Mexican society. Northern Mexico is influenced by the United States, but in ways that would not be particularly flattering to Americans. Mexicans are envious of the material wealth of the U.S., and they wish to borrow the technical knowledge that the U.S. has to offer. They do not want to give up their Mexicanness. They are oriented primarily to the things going on in Mexico and have little concern for the things going on in the United States, except for such things as how Mexicans are treated in the United States and what the United States thinks of Mexico. The penetration of American culture into Mexico is predominantly material through cultural diffusion, while the penetration of Mexican culture into the U.S. is predominantly linguistic, social, and ideological through migration.

Newly arrived immigrants from Mexico tend to be deeply involved in their own kinship systems, residentially segregated away from Anglo-Americans and uninvolved in formal U.S. organizations such as schools and political parties. However, their children, the second generation Mexican-Americans, tend to shift strongly toward an involvement with American culture—while still retaining Mexican ethnic social ties and identities. A continuing problem in this migration and adaptation situation is that the Mexican immigrants to the U.S. tend to be from the less educated and lower economic levels of Mexican society.

To estimate the degree of concern that the American and Mexican border populations have for each other, I measured the amount of newspaper space devoted to events in the alternate country or at the border itself. I compared 26 border-zone newspapers, 15 from the U.S. and 11 from Mexico, for their coverage of events or advertisements in the opposite country. The general finding of this survey was that there is extremely little coverage of events in the opposite country. Even in dual cities the people seem to almost ignore the events going on in the country across the border because it is culturally as well as nationally different.

The U.S. newspapers surveyed usually devoted less than 1 percent of their space to Mexico, Mexicans, or Mexican-Americans. The mean average was 0.7 percent. Six of the 15 newspapers had no Mexican content. For the three newspapers that had more than 1 percent Mexican content (Calexico *Chronicle*, Bisbee *Review*, and *Dispatch* [Douglas, Arizona]) most of the "Mexican space" was in paid advertisements for commercial enterprises in Mexico. All the Mexican newspapers had over 1 percent of their space devoted to U.S. coverage, primarily in advertisements paid by U.S. retailers and U.S. national news. The average was 2.8 percent, still very small, but four times the proportion of the Mexican coverage in U.S. newspapers. The single Mexican-American newspaper reviewed (*El Continental* [El Paso, Texas]) clearly reflected Mexican interest with 45 percent of content on Mexico and 25 percent on Mexican-Americans.

The border is initially only the physical line that divides two countries, but national interests create barriers and selective screens to control the movement of people, goods, and diseases. These screens are primarily responsible for the abruptness of the transition between Hispanic and Anglo cultures, for without them the transition would be gradual. From the point of view of the self-interest of the United States, the Mexican border screen for people is numerically efficient and qualitatively inefficient. That is, only a small number of Mexicans have been permitted to migrate to the United States, but those who have migrated tend to have been uneducated farm workers, domestic servants, housewives, and children rather than educated professionals.

The U.S. has not been a numerically significant "vent for Mexico's surplus population" or a "labor-escape valve" as some people have claimed. Only 3.6 percent (1.6 million) of the total known immigration to the United States since 1820 (45.5 million) has come from Mexico (U.S. Bureau of Census, 1972). Mexico now sends far more migrants into the U.S. than any other country (50,324 in 1971), but this is still only 13.6 percent of the total current immigration. Of the tens of thousands of wetbacks who attempt to immigrate illegally each year only a small proportion become successful, permanent immigrants, probably somewhat less than 1,000 a year. Mexico's population is currently increasing at about one and one-half million persons per year, so the U.S. receives a number equal to only about 3.3 percent of the total annual population increase, hardly a significant vent of surplus population. The U.S. screens on immigration are too protective to allow a really significant migration, legal or illegal.

Traffic at the border stations is a measure of U.S. tourism in Mexican border cities and of Mexican shopping and working in the U.S. A relatively small number of aliens making frequent crossings, particularly for shopping, constitute the bulk of the alien crossings. Surveys in Tijuana and Tecate (Price, 1967 and 1968) indicate that the average alien border crosser comes to the U.S. about once a week. Although there are more crossings of aliens, the U.S. citizen category involves several times as many individuals who make infrequent crossings, averaging probably only a few times a year. Thus, the individual U.S. citizen is more often a stranger and a tourist to the border situation than the Mexican resident.

In 1968 there were 136 million border crossings into the U.S. along the 2,013 miles of U.S.-Mexican border, 82 million by aliens and 54 million by U.S. citizens (U.S. Immigration and Naturalization Service, 1968). By state in 1967 there were 37 million into California, 19 million into Arizona, .3 million into New Mexico, and 72 million into Texas. The leading dual cities are ranked as follows by millions of entries: El Paso–C. Juarez, 31.9; San Ysidro–Tijuana, 22.6; Calexico–Mexicali, 12.9; Laredo–Nuevo Laredo, 11.4; Brownsville–Matamoros, 9.6; and Nogales–Nogales, 8.8. As a regular part of this border-crossing population about 44,000 aliens and 18,000 U.S. citizens (usually Mexican-Americans) resided in Mexico and commuted to their jobs in the United States in 1966 (see Samora, 1971: 21 for details on 1967).

The cities of northern Mexico are heterogenetic rather than orthogenetic, that is, they are creating original modes of thought rather than carrying forward the old cultural traditions. They are cities of a technical rather than a moral order. They are in a middle stage of industrialization with both light and heavy industries, with location near the raw materials and sources of power, and with a rapid expansion of social overhead facilities in power plants, highways, and such. The northern cities lack "quarters" or settlements populated primarily by migrants from particular districts of the country. However, stores, restaurants, bars, and streets are often named for the cities and states of interior Mexico. There are also associations like dance groups that represent particular Mexican states. The proliferation of common-interest associations is generally correlated with urbanization, and they are common in northern Mexico: commercial, historical, scientific, literary, and social.

The swift changes going on in the northern cities and

the problems of rapid urbanization are readily observable. Families migrating north with their few belongings are often seen along the northern highways. Men out of work sit around the city plazas or major intersections waiting for offers of day work. People still burn their trash openly in vacant lots and along the sides of the roads. Most of the roads are still unpaved, so that the air may be heavily laden with dust. There is still some construction of squatter's (*paracaidista*, "parachutist") shacks by the railroads, along highways, and on government lands generally. In the world of squatters there are tenants, landlords, speculators, and store operators, all on someone else's land. There are also self-imposed controls such as keeping the pathways open.

In their ethnography of El Paso—C. Juarez, D'Antonio and Form (1965) characterize the Mexican border town as including both a tourist and a regular business district with an immediate surrounding paved and patrolled residential district. Then beyond, in mixed and often deteriorated areas, are the factories, warehouses, adobe houses, tar-paper shacks, and vacant lots with broken or no paving and inadequate urban facilities.

The cities of the Southwest U.S. generally provide adequate facilities for potable water, sewage and garbage disposal, electricity, transportation, city zoning, education, and other basic urban problems. They are now bothered by a group of second-order urban problems such as juvenile delinquency, mental health, poverty, and ethnic conflict. Mexico's cities are still dealing with first-order urban problems such as potable water. In politics the Southwestern U.S. cities are run locally, efficiently, and economically, much like businesses, while in Mexico the heavy hand of the state and federal governments is felt in local politics. Thus, when city streets are to be paved in Mexico, the national political system becomes involved rather than merely a city council, engineers, and some contractors. Federal, state, and local police (each with separate criminal and traffic divisions) are simultaneously involved at the local level in the Mexican cities. Federal, state, and municipal governments, as well as private and church organizations, sponsor elementary schools.

The problems of northern Mexico's rapid urbanization are so great that it may take a national effort to solve them. Two federally backed programs, Programa Nacional Fronterizo and Departamento de Turismo, should play a crucial role in the development of northern Mexico. And in the long run northern Mexico is destined to play a key role in Mexico's future prosperity.

ii: *The Urbanization of Baja California*

Baja California is a semiarid peninsula almost 800 miles long with an average width of less than 100 miles. Throughout its early history it remained one of the most isolated and marginal areas of North America. Its arid climate has continually kept its population density low, and its isolation has meant that few changes have swept the peninsula (Price, 1971; Price and Smith, 1971).

For over 400 years, essentially since its discovery in 1533, Baja California was a land of Indians, missionaries, and struggling attempts at extractive industries such as pearling and mining. The desert climate and poor natural resources of this large peninsula has turned hundreds of commercial and colonizing attempts into failures, and the land is dotted with abandoned missions, mines, and towns. Even today driving the length of the peninsula is considered to be a great adventure by four-wheel drive vehicles because one traverses over 500 miles of unimproved dirt roads. Aided by clean air and the lack of a glow from city lights, the Institute of Astronomy of the University of Mexico operates a major observatory in Baja's San Pedro Martir Mountains at 9,200 feet above sea level. Most of the peninsula is still a rugged frontier in only tenuous communication with the modern world. Much of the interior is Sonoran desert with such strange plants as cirios, boojums, and elephant trees. However, this is not true of either the southernmost area around La Paz, the capital of the Territory of Southern Baja California, or the northernmost part of the State of Baja California along the U.S.-Mexico border. It is the urbanization of the northern arc that includes Ensenada, Tijuana, Tecate, and Mexicali that is now under examination. The following figures give the population of Baja California by municipio in 1970: Mexicali, 390,411; Tijuana, 335,125; Ensenada, 113,320; and Tecate, 17,917. In the large and rapidly growing cities of Mexicali and Tijuana only about one-third of the population was born in Baja California, but in Tecate and Ensenada the state-born proportions are higher at 44 percent and 50 percent respectively.

Banco Nacional de Mexico's *Review of the Economic Situation in Mexico* (1964) stated that

> The State of Baja California shows the highest standard of living, and the highest salaries in Mexico. . . . In 1960, this zone used 673 KwH of electric current per person (this was surpassed only by Nuevo Leon); it had 75 automobiles per 1,000 inhabitants (the Federal District had only 40); over 90% of the population in this zone were consuming bread . . . milk, fish, eggs, and wore shoes. Services to tourists are the main source of income, next are salaries earned by Mexican workers in the U.S. Such workers might work in Mexican industry but for the proximity of the U.S. and the long distance from centers of production in the rest of Mexico.

The prosperity of Baja California stands out when we compare it with Mexico City (Federal District) and Mexico generally. Mexico City is one of the world's great cities and exemplifies the extreme of urbanization in Mexico. Still, Baja California approaches the Federal District in many indices of urbanization, as Table 2 demonstrates (Dirreccion General de Estadistica, 1963, 1965A, 1965B, and 1966).

Baja California ranks very high in the percent of its population that is urban. It ranked second among the states of Mexico in terms of net population increase due to

TABLE 2

Comparisons of Baja California, Mexico City,
And All Mexico

	Baja California	Mexico City	All Mexico
Economically Active Population with a Monthly Income of 1,000 Pesos ($80.00) or Greater	55.7%	33.4%	15.4%
Areas of Employment			
Agriculture	29.4%		46.8%
Services	20.7		17.9
Manufacturing	20.5		15.8
Commerce	15.9		11.5
Others	13.5		8.0
Domestic Residences			
Average Number Rooms	2.0	1.9	1.7
More Than 50 Sq. Meters	40.4%	37.1%	36.3%
Drainage	26.9	89.5	26.9
Running Water	24.2	74.0	41.6

migration in the 1950-1960 period (Banco Nacional de Mexico, 1964: 8, 12). It has the highest average income in Mexico when only the economically active are considered. The 1970 census gave the very high figure of $1,045 per capita annual income in Baja California. It has a small proportion of the population in agriculture and large proportions in services, manufacturing, commerce, and other urban enterprises. The people of Baja California also have a significantly better education than Mexicans generally, about 85 percent of the children now completing the ninth grade. Baja California has about the best housing in Mexico in terms of number of rooms, space, and windows, but falls to or below the national average in proportion of dwellings with sewer drainage and running water.

Immigration

The first solid signs of an urban takeoff in Baja California appeared in the 1930s. In the decade of the 1930s the population increased 63.3 percent. Immigration then swelled into a great flood that almost tripled the population in the 1940s and doubled the population again in the 1950s. People continued to immigrate in the 1960s, and the population rose to 906,773 by 1970, 19 times the 1930 figures. At the same time there was a proportional shift of the population of Baja California into the cities from 45 percent in 1930 to about 80 percent in 1970.

From the 1950 and 1960 census figures it has been calculated that the majority of the migrants came from the western states, especially Jalisco (23.0 percent), Sinaloa (11.2 percent), and Michoacan (9.5 percent), Sonora (6.5 percent), Zacatecas (6.3 percent), and Guanajuto (6.3 percent) (Winnie, 1960). Most of these "source states" are in western Mexico, especially along the route of Highway 15. These states are communication and transportation links between Baja California and the rest of Mexico. Thus, people in these states are more responsive to opportunities in Baja California. Second, these states have had a long experience with urban migrations to such cities as Guadalajara and Mexico City because of displacement from farms due to population pressure on the land, mechanization of agriculture, and the lack of modern medical, educational, and service facilities in the rural areas. Thus, the migrants tend to have had some prior experience with town or city living.

The most widely applicable thesis about urban migration is that it is a response to a changing labor market. Social revolution has freed the peasant from land tenancy and made him responsive with increased economic expectations to an urban-based labor market. As wage levels in Baja California rose to the top in the nation, large numbers of workers, their families, and then later perhaps their relatives responded by migrating. To ease this migration was the relative abundance of unoccupied land in Baja California, the tolerance of "squatting" on government and even private land, and the democratic climate of a frontier where people are judged on ability rather than social origin.

Virtually universal problems arise wherever urbanization is extremely rapid: social services such as schools, hospitals, and public utilities are strained and inadequate; law and order is tested under the presence of recently arrived people of diverse cultural backgrounds and of many unemployed and transient persons, along with the building of shack towns on any accessible land. The latter is still evident in the outlying colonies in the hills surrounding Tijuana, along the bed of the Tijuana River, and along a canal outside Mexicali. Houses in these areas are made by the residents with scraps of wood, cardboard, tin, and tar paper. They usually have dirt floors and lack electricity, running water, and septic or sewer service.

Weak Integration with Mexico

A weak integration of Baja California with the rest of Mexico has been one of the dominant factors in its whole history. Its geographical separation as an isolated peninsula from the mainland of Mexico has meant that communication and transportation between Baja California and the rest of Mexico has been difficult and expensive. This has perpetuated its frontier character, while economic ties with the United States have become of great importance. This peninsula was the original California, before Alta California was discovered. The name came from the Greek words for beautiful (*kalli*) and bird (*ornis*). It was first used in an early Spanish fiction story for an island with Amazons and griffins "at the right hand of the Indies, very close to that part of the terrestial paradise and inhabited by women without a single man among them." The peninsula was for a long time considered to be an island.

The Spanish settlement and exploration of the peninsula moved at an extremely slow pace after its discovery in 1533. The peninsula was simply too arid. Alta California, on the other hand, had abundant natural resources and moved rather rapidly out of a later-starting frontier stage to become a well-integrated part of a new nation. Discovery of Baja California in 1533 was followed by over 300 years of exploration, missionary activities, epidemic disease among the Indians, and mostly abortive attempts at ranching, mining, pearling, and agriculture. From the 1840s until about 1940 there was a period of foreign commercial colonization and development companies, usually failures, and attempts to use Baja California as a base away from central Mexican government powers for revolution, for utopian communities, and for providing illegal goods and services to American tourists. These pressures and the fact that Mexico was weak at this frontier came close to drawing Baja California into the United States. By 1933 Baja California was moving rapidly to its current conditions. Prohibition was repealed in the U.S., to bring about a decline in the Baja California liquor industry. Baja California was then made a "free zone" for receiving American goods without customs taxes because of its distance from the markets of mainland Mexico.

General A. L. Rodriquez came to Baja California as the head of an army in 1920 and stayed to serve as governor between 1923 and 1929. In 1933, when he was interim President

   . . . he conceded the cities of Mexicali, Tijuana and Ensenada to be free *perimeters*, which meant that they had the privileges of bringing in foreign goods without the payment of duty. Later this

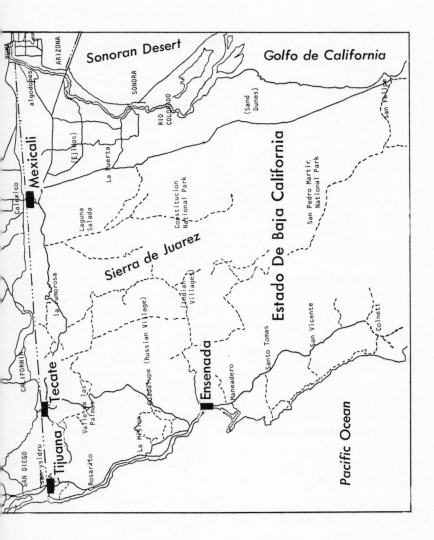

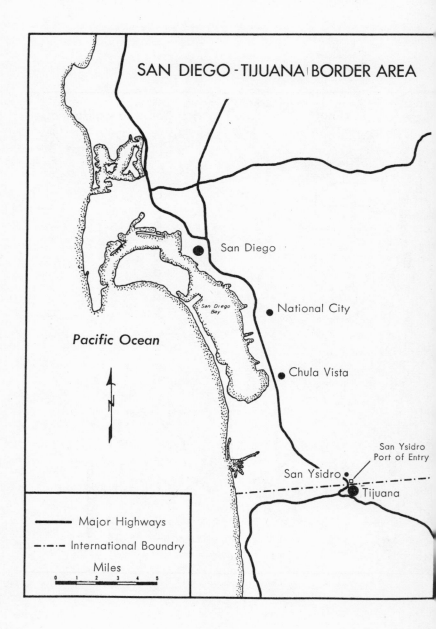

SAN DIEGO - TIJUANA BORDER AREA

San Diego

National City

San Diego Bay

Pacific Ocean

Chula Vista

San Ysidro Port of Entry

San Ysidro

Tijuana

——— Major Highways

—··—··— International Boundry

Miles

0 1 2 3 4 5

privilege was extended to the entire Peninsula. . . . Today this continues in force, but with many restrictions, since different articles have been removed from the list and those that may enter freely are relatively few (Martinez, 1960: 524).

This free-port status aids both the industry of tourism and the Mexican consumer in Baja California, because he does not have to pay Mexican duty on many consumer items such as most food and clothing and used cars that are five or more years old. Limitations come more from U.S. Customs regulations and California laws than Mexican regulations. Thus, for example, California state law prohibits the private importation of alcoholic beverages into California, although visitors from other states of the U.S. may bring one quart of an alcoholic beverage into California for consumption outside of California.

Another factor in the growth of Baja California is its proximity to California, the most populous state in the U.S., and to Southern California, the third largest industrial complex in the U.S. after New York and Chicago. With affluence and a fast freeway system people from Los Angeles drive to Tijuana for the races or a bullfight, some shopping, a meal at a Mexican restaurant, and drive back to Los Angeles the same day. The U.S. dollar is a major standard of exchange in Tijuana, and it is accepted without question in most of the rest of Baja California, an indication of the importance of tourism to the state.

While *political* ties to Mexico are very secure and feelings of Mexican nationalism are strong in Baja California, Baja California has stronger *economic* ties to the U.S. than to Mexico. More than one-half of the goods consumed in Baja California are imported, predominantly from the U.S. The following figures in Table 3 detail the average total monthly consumption of various products in tens of thousands of dollars in Tijuana and Mexicali in 1962 and the proportion of that consumption that was imported from outside of Mexico (Banco Nacional de Mexico, 1964).

TABLE 3

*Monthly Consumption of Foreign Products
In Tijuana and Mexicali*

	Consumption (X $10,000)	Percentage Imported
Transportation Equipment	114	99.9%
Paper and Paper Products	20	83.0
Machinery and Appliances	91	68.3
Other Manufactures	54	64.9
Food, Drinks, and Tobacco	644	62.7
Garments	91	58.8
Footwear	39	50.4
Non-Metallic Mineral Products	57	43.0
Metallic Products	57	42.7
Chemicals and Pharmaceuticals	161	40.3
Textiles	6	37.9
Magazines and Books	22	18.0
Fuels and Lubricants	199	12.8
Totals	1,555	54.0%

The Treaty of Guadalupe Hidalgo established the U.S.-Mexico border between Alta and Baja California. It technically fulfilled the Mexicans' demands for land access to the peninsula within their national borders, but in fact it did not provide a reasonable land access, so that today the highway from Tijuana must descend a winding road down an extremely steep escarpment into the Mexicali Valley. However, more important to history has been Mexico's tenuous political and economic control over the peninsula. An American, William Walker, with 45 men attempted to seize the peninsula in 1853-1854 to establish a "Republic of Sonora," but he was defeated by Mexican and American military forces. In the latter half of the nineteenth century various mining and colonization attempts were made in the peninsula largely with American capital. By 1890 foreign companies were in control of land concessions from the federal government that covered the majority of the peninsula. The two major foci of foreign colonization and commercial development were in the vicinity of Ensenada and Mexicali (Martinez, 1960).

Ensenada

In 1885 the Mexican government granted a charter of 16 million acres in northern Baja California to an American land-development company, the International Company of Mexico, incorporated in Hartford, Connecticut. This company turned Ensenada from a cattle ranch into a bustling town with cotton and woolen mills, a shoe factory, a distillery, a winery, soap and match factories, a tannery, and a cannery. The company subdivided Ensenada and sold lots of 6 1/2, 25, and 50 acres. Agriculture, animal husbandry, and mining boomed in the Ensenada region under the promotion of the American company. By 1887 the company claimed that 3,000 colonists had settled in their district of northern Baja California. However, President Diaz, who gave the grant, transferred the charter to a British firm that operated it from 1891 to 1917. Why the charter was transferred is still under debate. Brenton (1961) claims that it was because Diaz feared too much American influence on the border, while Martinez (1960) suggests an internal crises within the company, so that the company directors transferred their rights because of business considerations, but it is clear that nationalistic feelings in press reports of the time were strongly against these concessions. Among other things, the British built the first golf course on the North American continent at Ensenada.

The area was hit by a five-year drought from 1892 through 1896 and, except for a brief gold rush in 1889 and some outlying mining operations, the development project declined so greatly that there were only slight colonial vestiges left in 1906 when the federal government revalidated the concession until 1917. Ensenada folded into essentially a small fishing village between the turn of the century and the 1940s, when tourism began to play a major role in the town's prosperity. Hotel Playa Ensenada was a large gambling casino established in the 1930s that started the reputation of the town as a place with an ideal climate and facilities for sport fishing. Then, after 1955, a new deep-water port and related shipping facilities were constructed in Ensenada to handle the ocean-going transportation for northern Baja California (Anderson, 1964). The major international export from the port is long-staple cotton raised in the Mexicali Valley, but the port also sends out in coastal trade such goods as canned seafood products (from Ensenada) and beer (from Tecate). Into the port comes commercial fertilizer from Japan for the cotton fields, general merchandise from various ports of the world, and such coastal trade items as calcium carbonate (for cement), sugar, and livestock.

Today Ensenada is the second-largest coastal resort town in Mexico (after Acapulco), with the largest winery in Mexico (Santo Tomas), five large fish canneries, a lobster and abalone cannery, an olive packing plant, and a tannery. Ensenada is now just 60 miles south of Tijuana over a $26 million toll road that was opened in 1967. The toll of 30 pesos ($2.40) was set so high that Mexicans generally use the old road, but American tourists prefer the toll road, so that daily use has risen to about 3,000 cars weekdays and 5-6,000 on weekends.

Mexicali

Mexicali was the second area in northern Baja California to develop an urban concentration. Again, its growth was initially stimulated by American land developers. An irrigation project in the Imperial Valley of California extended over the border into the Mexicali Valley because of the technical needs for an impermeable soil base for the canal system. The year that water began to flow in this canal system, 1901, marks the beginning of Mexicali. Great stretches of land were controlled on the Mexican side by American firms at the time. By the end of the first decade of this century most of these parcels had been consolidated by the California-Mexico Land and Cattle Company. The company initially farmed north of the line and raised cattle south of the line, but soon began to parcel the land out to tenant farmers, particularly Chinese, East Indians, and Japanese. "By 1919, when the first large numbers of Mexican workers appeared, there were 5,000 Chinese farmers around Mexicali growing 80 per cent of the region's cotton, which was almost its only crop" (Chamberlin, 1951: 44-45).

The Chinese were very clannish, although a few did marry Mexican women and raise families in Mexico. They were harder workers and better organized than the Mexicans, so they tended to economically dominate the Mexicans, as the Chinese were in turn dominated by the American landowners. The Chinese would form cooperative companies with about 16 men and lease 1,000 acres of cotton land. All the men would then work the land for a share of the crop. In early Mexicali 14 of the 40 grocery stores, five of the ten dry-goods stores, and most of the eight hotels were owned and operated by Chinese.

The business success and immigration of Chinese came in conflict with the nationalistic sentiments of the Mexican Revolution. In the 1920s and 1930s the Chinese were ejected from their agricultural lands on one pretext or another and their stores were burned. In the Ensenada area in 1934 anti-Chinese riots developed when the Chinese were accused of mingling with Mexican women, hoarding money, and cutting prices to undersell Mexican dealers. More than 200 Mexicans burned a ranch that employed Chinese workers, and 13 Chinese stores were forced to close and sell out.

Several of the military and political events of the Mexican Revolution affected Baja California, but a major economic effect of the Revolution was the gradual wresting of the control of Mexicali Valley from American interests and the settling of the lands by Mexican nationals. Many Mexicans came into the Valley and settled as tenant farmers from 1919 on, 24,000 between 1919 and 1925, although many of these moved on to work and settle in the U.S. Under pressure from anti-Chinese agitation and Mexican nationalism, the company began to sell a few small lots in 1936 and finally thousands of 20 hectare lots in 1937 and 1938 to establish government-sponsored *ejidos*. By the end of 1937 38 *ejidos* had been established on 47,121 hectares of formerly American-held lands redistributed among 4,389 families in the Mexicali Valley (Chamberlin, 1951). The federal government finally bought out the remainder of the company's holdings in the Mexicali Valley in 1946. By that time Mexicali had developed into a large city that served as a commercial center for the agriculturalists in the Mexicali Valley. The railway that links it directly with mainland Mexico was completed in 1948.

> In its early years Mexicali was a "wide open" town, specializing in the types of vice calculated to attract the American tourists and ranchers of the Imperial Valley. The government, in order to finance its many material improvements . . . licensed gambling, prostitution, and opium refining. . . . About the only remainder of Mexicali's unsavory past is the relatively large number of bars and night clubs (Gerhard and Gulick, 1967:73).

While never a major tourist center, the city has developed as a major port of entry between U.S. and Mexico. Most of the truck traffic between the west coast of the U.S. and the interior of Mexico passes through Mexicali. Mexicali is the capital of Baja California and one of the large cities in Mexico, with a population now over 400,000.

There is still a squatter community along the Wisteria Irrigation Canal in Mexicali. People often move onto federally owned land such as this because the government is more tolerant of squatters than private landowners. Most of the people there are agricultural workers who have recently arrived from interior Mexico. Wisteria is a three-mile strip with 165 houses, mostly of adobe bricks or woven brush. Since they can be removed at any time, the people are not motivated to build better homes. The community has no electricity, piped water, sewers, or telephones. Most of the squatters have small vegetable gardens that they water by dipping from the canal. One man has nine cows, as well as pigs, goats, and chickens. Another man raises about 60 pigs. Children fish and swim in the canal. The community has two refreshment stands and a grocery store that receive some business from an adjacent highway. Wisteria also has a small fundamentalist Protestant church. Although the community has been in existence for several years, the people have been unable to get deeds to their land from the federal government.

San Felipe

San Felipe is 125 miles on a good paved road south of Mexicali. Its fame as a fishing port is based on certain conditions in the Gulf of California (Mexico calls it the Sea of Cortez). The water is warm and shallow, except for a long trench that parallels the peninsular coast. And the Colorado River is heavily laden with nutrients and silt. It deposits an average of 120 cubic meters of silt per second into the Gulf. The warm nutrient-filled water supports a rapid growth of plant and animal microorganisms upon which the shrimp and small fish feed, which in turn provide food for sea turtles and the larger fish: sharks, giant bass, guitar fish, ladyfish, Jack Crevalle, yellowtail, corvina, sole, and flounder. There are over 300 kinds of fish in the Gulf.

Totuava, a giant white sea bass (up to 200 pounds) found only off the coast of China and in the Gulf, was sought in the 1920s and 1930s for its bladders, which were dried and shipped to China for medicinal purposes. In the 1930s Americans began hauling totuava from San Felipe to the U.S. to sell for food. Sharks were also taken for their vitamin A-rich fins and livers. Then in the 1940s, realizing that the totuava stomachs usually contained about five pounds of shrimp, fishermen began to net shrimp and truck it to the U.S. This commerce led the Mexican government into building the road in 1950. When the road was completed, San Felipe began to boom as a tourist center for deep sea fishermen, since it cost so much less than fishing out of U.S. ports. A party of six can charter a boat for about $50 a day out of San Felipe, while it costs around $150 a day out of San Diego. With an average annual rainfall of only three inches, the weather around San Felipe is also good for flying.

Because so many people came in for shrimping, the Mexican government had to place seasonal limits on it, the season beginning each September 15. During the summer months the boats are put into drydock on the beaches for repairs. The rest of the time the shrimp boats (41 in 1968) must stay about one mile off shore because the Gulf has one of the highest tides in the world, averaging 20 feet in depth. These boats use 60- to 70-foot funnel nets and trawl slowly for four or five hours before each unloading of the net. A boat averages about 220 pounds per night, which is promptly packed in boxes with ice and then delivered to port every ten to 14 days.

The Use of Baja California by Californians

Although a greater proportion of the U.S. lives close to the U.S.-Canada border, more Americans make a regular use of Baja California than any other foreign territory. An average of about 35,000 Americans enter Mexico at the Tijuana border crossing each day. About 85 percent of these people are tourists destined for either Avenida Revolucion and other general tourism (40 percent); for the spectaculars such as horse racing, dog racing, bullfights, and *jai alai* (25 percent); or for Ensenada or parts of Baja California other than Tijuana (20 percent). The remaining 15 percent visit friends or relatives, have business in Tijuana, and so on. Persons in the latter category cross the border more often than others and would cross even more often than they do if it were not for the long wait and traffic jams that are part of entering the U.S. Over 90 percent of the cars driven by U.S. citizens that enter Tijuana have California license plates, so when I discuss Americans in Baja California I am primarily talking about Californians and their guests.

There are many small shops in Tijuana that advertise marriages and divorces, but these are only arrangement agencies. In marriages in Baja California each American citizen must have a tourist card. A marriage application is filed in Spanish at the civil registry of the city where the marriage is performed. Each party to the marriage must present a certificate of blood analysis and a certificate of physical examination performed by a laboratory in Baja California. Divorced persons must present proof of their divorce. If one party to the marriage is a Mexican citizen, authorization is required of the Mexican Immigration Department. The judge of the civil registry is the only person who can perform legal marriages.

It is very difficult for Americans to obtain a divorce in Baja California because both parties must have a tourist card, have six months of established residence in Baja California, and personally appear in court. However, divorce brokers in Tijuana can arrange for proxy, or absentee, divorce proceedings in a state in Mexico that has liberal laws, usually Guerrero, Morelos, Puebla, or Tlaxcala. Chihuahua used to be the major state for proxy divorces but recently outlawed them. Some states of the U.S. do not accept Mexican proxy decrees, and even the Mexican Supreme Court has cast some doubt on the validity of any proxy divorce. The Mexican Supreme Court ruled that matters regarding community property and custody of the children must be decided by a court in the place of residence of the parties to the divorce. Also, a study by the American Embassy in Mexico revealed that more than 30 percent of the divorce decrees from Morelos they had been asked to examine were fraudulent and without any record in the courts.

Californians go to the beaches of Baja California, especially in the Ensenada area. Sport fishing attracts Californians regularly to Ensenada on the Pacific Coast and San Felipe on the Gulf. The National Off Road Racing Association sponsors an 832-mile endurance race from Ensenada to La Paz in November each year and the "Baja 500" in June. A paved highway runs down the Pacific Coast for about 140 miles and then unpaved roads stretch for another 500 miles until the paved roads that run north from La Paz are reached. Baja California is used by tens of thousands of Californians as a vast park. Compared to 20 million Californians (about equal to one-half of the total Mexican population), this is not a high proportion of all Californians, but it still has a great impact on Baja California.

According to the Mexican Constitution foreigners cannot own real estate within 50 kilometers (31 miles) of a seacoast or 100 kilometers (62 miles) of an international border. Since Baja California is an extremely narrow peninsula (about 70 miles average width), this excludes most of the peninsula from foreign ownership. A center strip that averages only about eight miles wide would theoretically be open to foreign ownership. Still, by long-term liberal lease arrangements and the new interpretation of an old law (General Law of Titles and Credit Operations, Articles 346 to 350, allows foreigners to purchase property with usufruct, the right to use and enjoy) Californians are rapidly acquiring property rights along the coasts. The property is usually leased for 99 years and may be passed on to heirs without probate until the end of the lease. Between Tijuana and Ensenada homes are being erected and mobile homes and trailers are being moved in. Five major settlements of foreigners are operating in this stretch. A mobile home brought into Mexico needs no Mexican licensing and usually involves no import taxes when it is used as a residence. Foreigners who want to live in retirement in Mexico are given special considerations. There is a *pensionista* status for foreigners with permanent income which allows them to bring in their household goods, an automobile, and so on free from import duties.

It is quite difficult for foreigners to hunt in Mexico because of the various certificates and clearances hunters are supposed to have. To sport hunt in Mexico you should have the following: a tourist card, a hunting certificate from a Mexican consulate ($16.00 fee), authorization for the use of firearms in Mexico from the military commander nearest to port of entry (no charge, firearms must be checked out when leaving Mexico), a hunting license from the federal game warden nearest to your port of entry ($19.20 fee), and (with the above documents in hand) an Immigration and Customs Clearance at the port of entry.

iii: *Tijuana*
in Legend and History

The Legends of Tijuana

More Americans have visited Tijuana than any other Mexican city, probably over 60 million individuals in the city's history. In the press Tijuana is the classical "border town." Thus, Americans who have never visited Tijuana still know something of the legends of Tijuana.

The generation that goes back earlier than World War II to the Prohibition days might remember or have heard of Tijuana as beer gardens, slot machines in every bar, the luxury of prostitution houses such as the Moulin Rouge, and the excitement of celebrities like Jean Harlow, Clara Bow, or Al Capone visiting the elegant casino and race track at Agua Caliente. To many who visited during the 1940s it was a city of vice where prostitution, porno-graphic movies, live sex demonstrations, and drug traffic were unequalled. It was said to be a city where sailors could get roaring drunk, take over the bars, and fight in the streets with the marines.

Then there are more mundane parts of the story. The ice cubes in your glass and the vegetables in your salad might give you diarrhea, and "even the natives don't drink the tap water." The slightest automobile accident along the unpaved roads and in heavy traffic could land you in jail or at the least force you to pay a bribe to the police.

Things were cheap in Tijuana, and you could bargain the retailers down to ridiculously low prices. There were beggars in the streets, petty thieves, crowds of aggressive itinerant salesmen, pandering taxi drivers, and the sights and sounds of a dirty, garish tourist trap.

There is an undeniable base of reality in the legends. Tijuana has and continues to supply many goods and services which are illegal or more expensive in America. Being at the periphery or frontier of its own civilization, the border town tends to be relatively free from legal restraints, particularly when the town is small. What is illegal in one country may be a minor offense or even permitted in the other. For example, there is more tolerance of prostitution in Mexico than in the U.S., so that the Mexican federal law concerning prostitution does not apply to prostitution *per se* but to the procurer or pimp. U.S. law and moral standards have penetrated into the Mexican border cities to restrict the number of Mexican prostitutes and to make contact between American and Mexican prostitutes difficult, but has had little effect on the contact between Mexican men and Mexican prostitutes. While Mexico generally does not require a doctor's prescription for pharmaceutical items, the U.S. does. Thus, for a long time Americans were free to buy drugs in Mexico that would be restricted in the U.S. Due to U.S. pressure a prescription law and a dangerous-drugs law were recently passed by Baja California's state legislature. Along with "drunk and disorderly," "whereabouts," disrespect for a police officer, drug offense is one of the most common reasons given for the arrest of Americans in Tijuana.

The border is a meeting place of two civilizations, each, to the degree of their differences, exotic to the other. This difference between the civilizations leads to a mutually advantageous exchange of goods and services. The flow of goods and services may be so economically important that many ordinary laws are disregarded and a special informal "border town law" is created. The border-crossing station procedures seem to have evolved as a compromise between border town law and national law. Thus, the border officials use a loose working definition of national customs and immigration laws that emphasizes the spirit of the law more than the letter of the law. The border-crossing station is also separate from the border town in some ways. It is a special kind of neutral screening zone, analogous to a third country where only the police are the assured citizens and ordinary civil rights are abandoned, so that the border staff have a right to search a person's body and seize his goods without a warrant.

A final element in the American legends of Tijuana is the by-product of cultural shock by visitors to a foreign country. Compared to Canada, for example, Mexico differs greatly from the U.S., so that Americans understand the language and feel comfortable in English-speaking Canada while they are often confused and disoriented in Mexico. By staying in the tourist parts of Tijuana, where the signs and language are English, they can avoid most of the cultural shock, but then they come away with highly distorted ideas about the nature of Tijuana, one of the most common misconceptions being that Tijuana is not "really" Mexican. Except for the tourists themselves, the tourist street of Avenida Revolucion, the economic and social integration with the U.S., and the relative affluence of Tijuana, Tijuana is quite similar to other large northern Mexican cities. In broad cultural terms it is like Chihuahua or Monterrey, which is something like saying that Houston, Phoenix, and San Diego are similar southwestern U.S. cities. Like all of these cities, Tijuana is also unique in many specific ways.

The Mexicans have their own legends about Tijuana. Tijuana is a raw frontier, a place where social proprieties are blunted, where opportunities and hardships exist side by side. It is where people dare to challenge the political party (Partido Revolucionario Institucional) that has dominated Mexican politics for decades. Tijuana means better-paying jobs, and it is the door to the extremely high wages of the U.S. Moving to Tijuana means owning a car, a television set, and other appliances that are beyond the reach of most workers in the interior. The Mexican is ashamed of the vice in the city, believes that it is primarily for rich and jaded American consumers, and generally avoids association with it. Other elements in the American legends such as unpaved roads, graft, bad water, dirt, beggars, and high-pressure vendors are common in other Mexican cities and are thus simply not particularly a part of the Mexican legends.

Tijuana is an archtype of the international border town. It has the qualities of a free port-of-trade that is allowed to carry out certain specific functions that are illegal or not fully in the national interests of both nations, but is tolerated because of its overriding advantages to the two countries it serves. It is comparable to Hong Kong which, although it is a smuggling channel to Communist China, serves both the East and the West and thus is allowed to persist as a free port by both parties. When the threat of a border town to national interests becomes severe, the border can be closed to traffic, as has happened to the U.S.-Mexico border by both U.S. and Mexican action, but this is an unusual phenomenon. Even when there is war or extreme enmity between two bordering countries, there is some need for the reciprocal flow of goods, people, and information between the two countries. This history, then, is of the growth of a particular kind of urban structure. It is a case study of the creation of a border town and a port-of-trade.

While international trade and tourism became a basis for the growth of towns all along the northern frontier of Mexico, Tijuana was born solely of this trade and tourism. It has no history as a town prior to the creation of the border. Its natural resources would support only minor farming and ranching. And virtually no matter where the border was located within its present region a town of similar size and character as that of Tijuana would have developed.

Ranchero and Pueblo

The first entry of Europeans into the Tijuana River Valley was probably in 1769 when San Diego was first settled. In the early 1800's Jose Maria de Echeandia secured the rights and land from federal authorities to settle and operate a ranchero in northwestern Baja California. This was the beginning of Ranchero de Tijuana. Santiago Arguello received title to the Ranchero de Tijuana in 1829, probably because Echeandia had not properly promoted colonization of the area according to the 1824 Law of Colonization. By 1840 Ranchero de Tijuana was the largest of six cattle ranches in the area that collectively were considered a pueblo.

The name "Tijuana" is probably derived from two Spanish words: Tia and Juana, literally "Aunt Jane." A picturesque woman by this name came from Sonora as a cook and people referred to the area by her name (Cardenas, 1955). The area on both sides of the border was called Tijuana until the 1920s, when the name San Ysidro (a local ranch that dates back to 1873) began to be used for the U.S. side of the line. To distinguish between the two Tijuanas, the town on the Mexican side and south of the riverbed was called Old Town in the early 1900s. Also people in the U.S. tended to pronounce the "a" of Tia and spell Tia Juana as two words, while in Mexico the name was pronounced Tijuana, with a guttural Spanish "j" sound, and they spelled it as one word. Some Mexicans thought it was degrading to have a name like Aunt Jane for their town. Thus, in 1925 the Mexican Congress renamed it Ciudad Zaragosa, but this was met with opposition, so that Emilio Portes Gil, the Mexican President, had the name changed back to Tijuana in 1929.

In 1848 negotiations over the location of the U.S.-Mexico border ranged from leaving California in Mexico to giving Baja California to the U.S. Mexico said that Baja California was poor in natural resources and of no importance to the U.S., that Mexico needed Baja California for the strategic defense of Mexico, and that Mexico also needed a land communication route between Baja California and the Mexican mainland. Thus the final draft of the Treaty of Guadalupe read

> And to avoid all difficulty in tracing on the land the limits that separate Upper and Lower California, it is agreed that the limit should consist in a straight line drawn from the middle of the Gila River, at the point where it meets the Colorado, to a point on the Pacific Coast, one marine league distant to the south of the most southerly point of the port of San Diego, according to the drawing of this port which the second pilot of the Spanish armada, D. Juan de Pantoja, made in 1782. . . .

The resulting line cut diagonally across the Tijuana River Valley, leaving the mouth of the Valley on the U.S. side and the narrowing upper part of the Valley on the Mexican side. The line also made Tijuana the most distant point within the Republic from the national capital, 1,845 miles.

In 1871 U.S. officers were appointed to patrol the border area. A few years later customs officials were stationed at the border itself, operating at first out of a general store just on the American side and then at the border official's home. A small U.S. customs house was built in the early 1900s.

A Mexican customs port was established in 1874 at Tijuana to collect revenue on the traffic headed toward Ensenada. Charles Nordhoff (1888) lauded the colonial opportunities in Baja California, particularly in the Ensenada area, and wrote that the colonists may bring in duty free all that they need to establish themselves such as goods for housing, furniture, tools, provisions, animals, and so on. However, goods paid high duties when ordinarily imported. These duties were collected primarily at Tijuana.

In March 1889 there was a brief rush of Californians to reported rich gold fields in the Santa Clara and El Alamo areas, southeast of Ensenada. Some 2,000 arrived, took an estimated $20,000 of gold out by panning, and spent an estimated $250,000 in the process. The Mexican customs officials at Tijuana seem to have milked this group of travelers for as much as the traffic could bear.

> Many who went to the line . . . were brought up short at the Tia Juana customhouse, and unless their papers were made out in order, and their manifests correct, and their bonds for geldings and vehicles satisfactory, a cash deposit was demanded as a guarantee that the stock admitted would be brought back out again or the duty paid thereon. . . . By the first week in March several hundred were stalled at the border (Lingenfelter, 1967: 13-36).

A newswriter in the Santa Clara camp said that one party paid $24 duties on $25 worth of provisions. Another man paid $13.62 duty on a saddle worth $1.

A writer for *The Nation* cited by Ridgely (1966: 58) visited the town in 1889. "There are more saloons in Tijuana than buildings. . . . Some are in tents, open in front, with a counter in the center and empty beer barrels for seats." In the 1880s the Tijuana Hot Springs Hotel was built at Agua Caliente, two miles southeast of the border station. It was washed out by the floods of 1891 and then reopened in 1915 with claims to being a modern Turkish bath with an orchestra and day and night entertainment. About 1906 John D. Spreckels built a railroad from San Diego to Yuma, Arizona, that crossed the Mexican border and had stations in Tijuana and Tecate. This railroad helped to tie Tijuana in the early days much more closely to the U.S. than to the distant Mexican interior.

The frontier location and character of Tijuana played a role in the Mexican Revolution. The Mexican Liberal Party, under the brothers Ricardo and Enrique Flores Magon, in 1910 fought the dictatorship of Porfirio Dias as well as the more important party of Francisco I. Madero. The Liberal Party had been forced to shift its base of operations out of Mexico to Los Angeles, had allied with the International Workers of the World, and mounted an attack from outside of Mexico. The Liberals took the town of Mexicali, captured Tecate, and moved on and captured Tijuana after battles on May 9 and 10, 1911. Tijuana was defended in the battles by about 100 men, some of whom were paid American mercenaries. The Liberals, now composed of about 50 percent Americans, many of them from the International Workers of the World movement in the U.S., and some Kiliwa Indians, planned next to march on Ensenada, but the Mexican dictator Diaz was beaten by the forces of Madero in central Mexico, and he signed the Treaty of Juarez in which he promised to resign and leave the country. The Liberal Party was not in agreement with the program of Madero and still planned to march on Ensenada until the Liberal general in Tijuana, Carlos Rhys Pryce, an American, deserted on May 30, taking Liberal funds with him. This left Jack Mosby in charge.

The federal forces arranged for the Liberals to lay down their arms in Mexicali and moved on to Tijuana. The federals then sent a message to Jack Mosby to come to the international line. While they were talking of a peaceful settlement, the federal forces attacked and took Tijuana.

> In order to attack the frontier town, Celso Vega had organized a body of auxillary volunteers among the local people and Mexicans who had crossed over from the United States. . . . Vega assembled more than 600 men and had two machine guns; and in a short battle on June 22, he dislodged the socialists. . . . In the hour of action there were about 500 rebels in Tijuana, of which 31 were killed and many were wounded (Martinez, 1960: 483).

Many people came down from San Diego to watch the battle from the hills on the U.S. side. Baja California was kept out of further severe revolutionary battles by the strong governor of the Territory of Northern Baja California, Esteban Cantu.

The entrenchment of relatively stable modern government in Baja California began in 1915 when Colonel Cantu became governor of the northern district. His officials collected all federal taxes, and even collected duties on all national merchandise that entered the territory, just as foreign goods were taxed. They imposed a personal tax and licensed gambling houses. Cantu's administration expanded the economic development of the Mexicali Valley. It built schools and federal and municipal government buildings, and generally improved Mexicali. Cantu's regime was forcefully ended in 1921 under rumors of the separatism of Baja California, excess taxes, a costly administration, and some graft and nepotism (Martinez, 1968: 510ff.). After four brief-term governors, General Abelardo C. Rodriguez took over the territorial government from 1923 to 1926. His administration prospered with the great increase in tourism and the sale of alcoholic beverages during the U.S. Prohibition, especially in Tijuana. He promoted colonization of the territory by Mexican nationals and distributed lots of land to farmers. In 1925 he created the municipality of Tijuana.

Ciudad de Turismo

In 1915 Tijuana had a population of about 1,000. Tourists who had come to see the San Diego Exposition of 1915-1916 came touring to Tijuana by steam dummy in open cars. One traveler said it consisted of just

> a number of wooden stores, restaurants, and saloons, mostly one-story, with a scattering of wooden bungalows, some neat and whitewashed, on the side streets. All streets (are) . . . dusty and often rutty and, in wet weather very muddy but . . . wide.

Another man said, "There were just a few Mexicans in ponchos and serapes sitting on their haunches" (Ridgely, 1966: 58). Despite this picture of a sleepy town, Tijuana began to awaken to modern life in 1915. It had over 100 houses, a church, a primary school, and the customs station.

Antonio Elousa was issued the first gambling license in Tijuana on July 15, 1915, and he built the Tijuana Fair in the Old Town of Tijuana. The Fair was a gambling casino and bar with a variety of side attractions such as bullfighting, cock fighting, boxing matches, musical groups, and free barbecues. Both boxing and horse racing had been banned in California and several other states at the time.

James Cofforth, a former boxing promoter from San Francisco, started his first 100-day-racing-season program in Tijuana on January 1, 1916. He had built a racetrack one-quarter of a mile south of the border station. This was convenient to both those who drove down by car and those who came by train. The racetrack had stables for 100 horses and grandstands that could seat 3,500 people. Cofforth's plan was to charge $1 admission, to derive $120 daily from each of an estimated 15 bookmakers for an income of $1,800, and to make $100 a day from the bar and $50 a day from the program concession. A few weeks after it opened, on January 18, 1916, the track and Tijuana was flooded out. The automobile bridge across the Tijuana River was washed out. When the first racing meet was ended on July 24, 1916, Cofforth set to work expanding and improving the track facilities: more stables, a dike to protect the track from further floods, beds of flowers, and improved roads near the track.

The racetrack's major competition, the Tijuana Fair, added the $100,000 Monte Carlo casino between the border and the track. This was a 24-hour cabaret, casino, and restaurant that featured such entertainment as a group of Mexican dancers and an Irish quartet.

World War I was stirring the country, and a moral reform movement was intensifying. Prostitution was forced out of San Francisco's Barbary Coast in February 1917, and San Diego began to prohibit dancing in cabarets. On June 18, 1917, a Friendship Fiesta was held in Tijuana in which the governor had 32 steers barbecued and served in the racetrack. This fiesta was meant to help solidify relations between Mexico and the U.S. that were being strained by the different positions of the two countries on the war in Europe and the moralistic disdain of some people in the U.S. for the freedom of the border towns. The fiesta had little effect on the growing pressures within the U.S. In June 1917 men in U.S. military uniforms were forbidden by the U.S. to enter Mexico. In San Diego at the time there was an Army camp at Kearny Mesa and a new naval air station on North Island. Then in December 1917 the U.S. Immigration Department began to require passports for anyone to enter the U.S. Immigration officials declared that

> Tijuana as a tourist town for Americans will cease to exist during the war. Pleasure-seekers, tourists and in fact men and women in every walk of life are absolutely permitted from crossing the border unless their business is such as to render their presence in Mexican territory imperative.

On July 1, 1917, Elousa sold his gambling permit to Carl Withington and Ed Henderson.

Three cabaret operators who were pressed out of the Bakersfield, California area by a reform movement went to Mexicali in 1913 and founded The Owl and then the Tivoli Bar in Tijuana. Their names were Marvin Allen, Frank B. Byer, and Carl Withington, and they formed the ABW Corporation. These three men plus Baron Long, of racing fame in Los Angeles before racing was closed down there, and James Cofforth, the boxing promoter from San Francisco, formed the major financial powers in Tijuana from this time into the 1920s. The ABW Corporation was a major financial source for the Tijuana racetrack, and it held the gambling license that had been purchased from Elousa and held under special arrangement with Governor Cantu. The property at the time of the track's construction was owned in part by John D. Spreckels, the sugar and rail financier. Cofforth handled the racing, Withington handled the gambling, and Ed Baker controlled the importing of spirits into Tijuana and Mexicali, and with Withington ran the Mexicali Brewry.

When the international border first reopened after World War I those who crossed were still required to have passports. Mexican visas were issued without charge at the office of the Mexican consul in San Diego, but Mexico's policy at the Baja California border changed from week to week. Without a practical passport arrangement, traffic to Tijuana was so small that there was no 1919 racing season in the town. Shut down during World War I, the track reopened in January 1920, the same time that prohibition of alcoholic beverages went into effect in the U.S. On January 16, 1920, the 18th Amendment to the U.S. Constitution, the Volstead Act, went into effect. This became the greatest single boon to Tijuana, since it was still quite legal to drink in Mexico.

Jack Dempsey served as honorary race starter on opening day. Charlie Chaplin, Fatty Arbuckle, Tom Mix, Buster Keaton, and other movie stars of the day began to grace the Tijuana scene. Before the racing meet of 1920 was a month old, the Sunset Inn opened near the track in a $20,000 extension of the old Monte Carlo Club, where gambling was still held. On July 4 of that year an estimated 65,000 people came to Tijuana. So many cars were used for the weekend travel that San Diego "ran out of gas" and had to ration fuel to only essential vehicles. Still, the customs and immigration checkpoint was only one car wide, and the gate into the U.S. closed at 10:00 p.m. No passports or other documents were required at the checkpoint.

A writer for the *New York Times* (Ridgely, 1966-1968: IV: 117) had these impressions of Tijuana in 1920.

> ... a recrudescence of a Bret Harte mining camp or a Wild West main street scene in the movies, with a dash of Coney Island thrown in.... On either side is a succession of saloons, dance halls, moving picture barns and gambling dens.... The air reeks of dust, warm humanity, toilet perfume, stale tobacco.... The welkin rings and vibrates with the laughter and chatter of abnormal good spirits, the noise of an occasional fracas ... the roulette wheel ... the tap-tap-tap of hammers where new joy palaces are being shot up overnight to accommodate the business of the prohibition boomtown, and, above all, the continuous jangle of jazz.... The gambling? Every form of it invented by man.... Even the humble shell game, playing openly on the

sidewalks . . . the sort of life that once made the Bowery famous. . . .

The Board of Temperance, Prohibition, and Public Morals of the Methodist Church in 1920 (Ridgely, 1966-1968: VI: 45) wrote

> Everything goes at Tia Juana. There are scores of gambling devices, long drinking bars, dance halls, hop joints, cribs for prostitutes, cock fights, dog fights, bullfights. . . . The town is a mecca of prostitutes, booze sellers, gamblers and other American vermin.

While Governor Cantu was being forceably replaced by the federal government between August 12 and 21, 1920, the Tijuana border crossing was closed, except for a special agreement that allowed American Legion conventioneers in San Diego to visit Tijuana. When no other town on the Mexican border was imposing such charges, the Mexican immigration officials quoted a $10 charge for a "passport" and $2 for a ten-day visitor's permit. On February 21, 1921, the Lower California Jockey Club called off racing to force the Mexican immigration officials to ease up on the charge. On March 3 U.S. President Woodrow Wilson helped by repealing the U.S. passport charge. Then on March 10 James Cofforth of the Jockey Club said that decreased Mexican passport charges allowed the racing meet to continue. The U.S. government at the time was investigating the traffic in narcotics from Tijuana and Mexicali, while the Mexican federal government tried to rule that foreign currency would no longer be honored in Mexico. Then a shooting incident six miles south of Tijuana closed the border for about a week in November 1921. Trouble arose between the track and the local government when Mexican officials began to charge a 25-cent toll on each auto that passed over the road to the racetrack, although the track had built the road and it was on racetrack property. The same year saw the invention of the photo finish at the Tijuana track.

Arson and accidental fires were common in Tijuana in the 1920s. Almost all of the construction was of wood, and sawdust was thrown on the floors of the bars. Bars burned down from time to time, and fire destroyed part of the racetrack's stables on November 24, 1924. About one-third of the town's saloons were destroyed in a fire in the fall of 1922. For over a century the ownership of the ranch and city of Tijuana rested primarily within the Arguello family. They had taken over the land grant of Jose de Echeandia, colonized and promoted civil development, and thus had become the legal owners. Then, under a legalism of land reform the ownership of the property was simply returned to the Republic of Mexico in 1923 for popular distribution.

The racetrack was supposed to pay $2,000 per racing day in taxes, which with a 100-day season would be $200,000 a year. The ABW Corporation's gambling concession for Mexicali and Tijuana, irrespective of the racetrack, was rumored to cost $65,000 a month in 1924, but this had to be renegotiated with the state government every year. The partnership that encompassed the Owl Cafe in Mexicali and in Tijuana the Tivoli Bar, Foreign Club, Sunset Inn, Monte Carlo, and the racetrack also was called on to help pay for the construction of roads and other civic improvements.

In 1924 the Sunset Inn was a large casino with fourteen games of 21, eleven roulette tables, ten crap tables, four chuck-a-luck outfits, two poker tables, and two wheels of fortune. There were often more than 1,000 people in the casino room. Attached to this was the Monte Carlo bar, and both were connected to the racetrack and the railway station by a covered wooden runway. A half mile away was Old Town, about 200 yards in length with a hotel, a curio shop, and 65 saloons. The saloons had staffs of young American bar hostesses from Southern California to keep the men buying drinks and to serve as dime-a-dance partners. Some of these girls were also prostitutes. The saloons had "one-arm bandit" slot machines, beer by the pitcher, free peanuts and pretzels, and "large crowds on small dance floors." Each saloon was supposed to pay a minimum tax of $1,000 a month and $2 tax per bottle of liquor sold. Most of the owners and employees were U.S. citizens, a situation that created great resentment among the Mexicans. For example, in 1923 about 50 Mexicans stormed the Tivoli Bar and overturned the gambling tables to protest the discriminatory employment of U.S. citizens over Mexicans. A lady banjoist broke her banjo in the fight. At its peak in the 1920s the Foreign Club employed 19 Americans and one Mexican as bartenders.

In March 1924 the U.S. government yielded to reform pressures and began to close the border stations at 9:00 p.m. The governor of the Mexican territory filed a formal protest, but it backfired on him when the Mexican federal government shut down all border gambling for a period, except at the racetrack. The governor had shut down gambling himself in 1921. Stopping the gambling became an off-and-on political power maneuver. In fact, it was against the law for Mexicans to gamble in Tijuana except at their own poker clubs.

In 1926 the Casino de Agua Caliente was built on the site of the abandoned Tijuana Hot Springs Hotel. It had long mirrors, chandeliers, and walls of rose brocade. It had large ornate rooms, in one of which, the Salon de Oro, gambling was only in gold coins. The passport situation had been settled in favor of the tourist, so that no passports or other documents were required for Americans. Then the beautiful Agua Caliente Spa was constructed of the finest Italian tile in 1930. It had fountains and a public lobby with small shops. The complex had a great hotel and rows of bungalows. It was landscaped with grass, walkways, and rows of palm trees. In 1930 the Agua Caliente Open with $25,000 in prize money was the richest tournament on the professional golfing circuit. This drew the best golfers of the day to Tijuana. Old Town claimed the "world's longest bar" of 200 meters on Avenida Revolution. Down the street from that at the Foreign Club they say that Tom Mix used to fill his hat with 25-cent and 50-cent pieces and throw them to the children in the streets. While bullfighting was prohibited in the U.S., it drew large crowds in Tijuana. The Rodriguez Dam was built on the Tijuana River in 1928 to help prevent the town's perennial drought and flood cycles.

In 1927, during the height of the U.S. Prohibition, the Caesar Salad was invented in Tijuana. Alex Cardini, his brother Caesar, and an associate, Paul Maggiora, ran a fashionable Italian restaurant on Avenida Revolucion. Alex had been a pilot in the Italian Air Force in World War I and thus had many friends who were pilots for the U.S. stationed at Rockwell Field at North Island in San Diego. As a cook in Tijuana he created a unique salad that used grated Parmesan cheese, boiled egg, garlic, olive oil, lemon juice, anchovy paste, and fried bread croutons over lettuce. He called it the Aviator's Salad, but as the reputation of their food spread, his brother's name, Caesar, became associated with their salad. The following are the ingredients of the original salad, according to Alex Cardini.

1 cup French bread croutons
1/3 cup olive oil
2 cloves garlic
1-2 tsps. anchovy paste
1 bunch romaine lettuce
salt and pepper to taste
juice of 1 lemon
1 tsp. Worcestershire sauce
1 coddled egg

Depression, War Years, and the New Complex City

The repeal of Prohibition and the stock market crash of October 1929 and the subsequent Depression in the U.S. was a hard blow to the border towns. The first year that the number of border crossers at the San Ysidro station was counted was fiscal 1931, with 5,426,034 persons, over 90 percent of them U.S. citizens. Traffic decreased after that and was not over 5 million again until after World War II in 1946. The Depression cut so heavily into their revenue that many Mexicans left for other parts of their country. To help offset the Depression in Baja California a free-trade zone without import duties was put into effect for Tijuana and Ensenada on August 30, 1933, extended to Mexicali, Tecate, and San Luis Rio de Colorado in 1935, and then to all of Baja California in 1939. This trade-free status was gradually taken away, as item after item was taken off the free-import list. It still includes most of the things that are simply for resale to tourists.

The Moulin Rouge (French for "red mill") was the most famous house of prostitution in early Tijuana (on Madero and Seventh, now a school) with lavish interiors, girls of all races, and a miniature red mill on the roof. It was owned by a Japanese man. The name in Spanish translation, Molino Rojo, was taken over by two bars in Tijuana and one in Ensenada. In 1968 the Molino Rojo on Avenida Constitution and Calle Coahuila had about 50 girls who served as prostitutes, in addition to their jobs as bar girls, dancers, and demonstrators in live sex acts. Along with a few private homes in Zona Norte, the Molino Rojo also showed lewd movies where the prostitutes came in to caress the male viewers to set up contracts.

The racetrack was closed down, and the Mexican anti-gambling law was enforced in 1935. Victor Peñalosa, who worked at Casino de Agua Caliente in the early days, said that Italians, Greeks, and Americans, as well as Mexicans, owned the clubs in those days. They had their clubs insured, and when it became clear how bad business was going to be, they burned them down for the insurance. He said that there were about 20 bad fires in downtown Tijuana in 1935. After that, most of the foreign owners left town, and some of the bars became curio shops. And the casino dealers, who were used to making $25-$30 a night, went on to work as common laborers at four pesos a day. They had Stetson hats; Hart, Shaffner and Marx suits; and Florsheim shoes; and they believed the money would never stop. Then suddenly they were out on the street without a job.

With drinking legalized in the U.S. and gambling closed in Mexico, the U.S. border station at San Ysidro relaxed its midnight closing time and went to a 24-hour operation. In 1937 the racetrack reopened, but other forms of gambling were still held as illegal. Gambling is legal today in Tijuana in connection with dog racing, *jai alai*, and the national lottery, in addition to horse racing. The jai alai fronton, or playing court, was started in the early 1930s during the days of open gambling, but building was stopped when gambling became illegal, and then it was finally completed in 1946. Greyhound racing was added to the Agua Caliente horse-racing track in 1947 by construction of a special portable 5/16 of a mile track for the night racing of dogs.

When President Lazaro Cardenas closed down the last gambling center, Casino de Agua Caliente, on July 20, 1935, this lavish complex of casino, hotel, bathing resort, and gardens became a technical high school. Tourism decreased, but it was also the end of the era of U.S. dominance in Tijuana's business. While U.S. capital played a moderate role in the boom of the 1940s, Mexican businessmen were in control, and the proportion of their control increased to such an extent that today the only prominent U.S. businessmen in Tijuana are the managers of Woolworth de Mexico and the racetrack.

In the war years of the early 1940s Avenida Revolucion was still downtown Tijuana with residences immediately surrounding it. Cattle grazed on the Agua Caliente golf course. There was little development in the barren, dry hills until the 1950s. While the 1930s had brought depression to the town, the town became a booming entertainment center again in the 1940s. As one person said of Tijuana in the 1940s, "everyone from eight to eighty is in business."

A Mexican informant said:

During the war we had thousands of sailors in their uniforms every night. They came with a few months pay and spent it wildly. We figured the Americans were real suckers. They would order shots of tequila with beer chasers and in an hour they were yelling in the streets. The girls in town were afraid to go near Avenida Revolucion. That's when the hawkers began yelling "Come in! Come in!" and the tourists and the strippers came in.

Gerald Mokma, the U.S. consul in Tijuana during the war years, told about Tijuana's early reactions to World War II. Immediately after December 7, 1941, the Mexicans, who did not declare war on the Axis powers until May 1942, rounded up all Japanese, Germans, and Italians and sent them to the interior. They told them not to go to the coast. When the U.S. called for a local blackout to avoid presenting a target for potential Japanese bombers, San Diego was lighted brightly, while Tijuana turned the power off over the whole city. To squelch rumors about the Japanese building landing strips and ammunition dumps in Baja California for an attack on California, 40 U.S. soldiers and their officers in civilian clothing were taken on a tour of Baja California by the Mexican army. One of the first acts of the U.S. government was to briefly close off the border to entry from Mexico, but since Baja California was so dependent upon Southern California for many essentials, more than 100 key people were given special permits to cross regularly. The border was then opened, but there were special precautions to prevent German nationals, written materials, and U.S. currency (there was a $250 limit) from leaving the U.S.

Tijuana played a unique role in the face of the scarcities and rationing of World War II by 1944 (Zahn, 1944: 14-15).

Tijuana's new clientele is mostly Army, Navy and aircraft workers. . . . They are trying to buy everything that has become extinct in the States . . . they can buy alarm clocks, meat, gasoline, butter, cream, shoes, woolens, hardware, sporting goods, silk stockings, chewing gum, and yes — hairpins.

Tires had sold out fast, gasoline was actually limited to 16 liters per vehicle with a permit, and it took U.S. Office of Price Administration ration coupons to buy shoes and meat.

> Washington officials . . . could keep Tijuana employees from commuting to work in San Diego and stop San Diego merchants from operating stores in Tijuana . . . (but) bordertown is a suburb of San Diego, and little more than a colony operated by American citizens. That is one reason why its families are given genuine OPA ration books. The main reason for the plan is that Tijuana merchants sold so many rationed items to U.S. shoppers that the native stocks became scarce. Today, through a fantastic arrangement, Mexican families drive across the border to San Ysidro, California and buy from U.S. chain stores.

In 1942 the Bracero Program was started, initially to alleviate the shortages of farm workers as men were drawn into military and defense plant work. Later it was continued on beyond the end of the war as a source of cheap labor. In time this program brought hundreds of thousands of contract agricultural workers from Mexico to work in the U.S. The Bracero Program was terminated at the end of 1964, but it had greatly stimulated migration to the U.S. and to northern Mexico.

In 1952 and 1953 San Diego's district attorney, Donald Keller, and others launched an eventually successful program to restrict entry of unchaperoned individuals under 18 years of age into Mexico. As part of this campaign Keller turned a list of 16 abortionists over to the Tijuana authorities. One writer reported in 1952 that an estimated 600 people under 18 years of age crossed the border into Tijuana each week without their parents, that the city had an estimated 3,000 prostitutes, that marijuana peddlers were common, that pornographic literature was readily available, and that abortionists have agents who look for customers. The San Diego City Police now operate a checkpoint at the entrance to Tijuana to keep teenagers without written permission from their parents or proper chaperones from entering Mexico. About 13,000 teenagers are turned away from crossing into Mexico at this point each year, more than 80 percent of them from outside of San Diego County.

Today Tijuana has only a few hundred prostitutes who deal with foreigners, there are very few marijuana peddlers and these are primarily peddlers of bulk quantities for export to the U.S., the sale of pornography has been eliminated, and abortion is less common than in California. With urbanization and industrialization there has been a move in the direction of middle-class puritanism. Pornographic literature and abortions are now much more readily available in the U.S. than in Mexico.

On January 25, 1959, Mexican soldiers and federal police raided the gambling casino at Rosarito Beach Hotel and took more than 30 American prisoners. They were treated rather roughly and bail was set at from $400 - $1,600. This raid helped to spread the fear of the capriciousness of Mexican law and depressed the amount of tourism in Baja California in 1959. Over 10,000 Americans are arrested annually in Tijuana, usually for misdemeanors such as being drunk and disorderly, vagrancy, and unlawful possession of pills, which typically involve only a $24 fine. However, a few Americans are convicted and sent to the Mexican prison for such crimes as armed robbery, rape, and murder. The bars and brothels with their predominantly young or military or college-student clientele are still there, but they have gradually declined in relative importance in the face of the growth of family tourism and industrialization. Street-walking girls and pandering taxi drivers are being pushed off the streets by the crowds of wives and children searching for good bargains in the souvenir shops.

The 1960s have been marked by the transition of Tijuana to a large, industrialized city, whose products now include hosiery, wigs, cigarettes, furniture, transformers, radios, canned goods, and many others. Yet tourism is still the largest industry, and it continues to grow each year, although its relative importance has declined as manufacturing and services have increased at a greater rate than tourism.

The character of Tijuana has shifted widely over its history. In the nineteenth century it was a ranching center, while by 1889 the customs house, the saloons, and the hot-springs resort were a distinctive part of the Tijuana scene. The 1915-1916 Exposition in San Diego brought thousands of tourists to San Diego and many of these crossed over to Tijuana, particularly for its gambling. As moral reform became stronger in the U.S., Tijuana became an increasingly important source for rough male entertainment. After 1945 and the end of World War II Tijuana began to add the new dimensions of manufacturing and family tourism. These new "tourists" from California come to shop for Mexican crafts, furniture, clothing, and so on. They are not very interested in sight-seeing. Horse racing, bullfighting, and *jai alai* became respectable spectaculars. Saloons, while still present, declined in relative importance to souvenir shops selling arts and crafts.

Tijuana is now a modern oriented city. The pace of life is fast. People are active in sports events, social clubs, and politics. They are literate, driving, and dedicated to creating a great future for Tijuana. They are also aware of the special problems that Tijuana has as a border town and as a port-of-trade, a set of conditions that can foster economic growth with open border and free-trade policies.

Border-Crossing Patterns at Tijuana-San Ysidro

Border-crossing patterns reflect international cultural relationships over time. Thus in a long view, from 1934 to 1969, we see the gradual growth of the San Ysidro port-of-entry into a station with one of the largest volumes of traffic in the world: over 27.3 million crossers in 1969. This reflects the growth of extremely strong symbiotic relations between northern Baja California and southern California.

BORDER CROSSINGS 1934-1969, SAN YSIDRO, CALIFORNIA

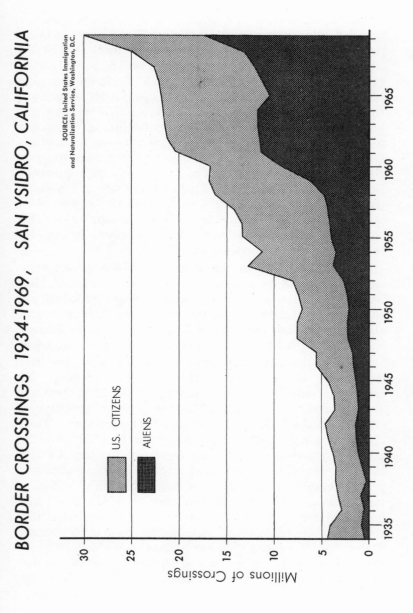

SOURCE: United States Immigration
and Naturalization Service, Washington, D.C.

U.S. CITIZENS

ALIENS

Millions of Crossings

30
25
20
15
10
5
0

1935 1940 1945 1950 1955 1960 1965

The limitation of movement due to different positions of the United States and Mexico on World War I; a boom due to prohibition and moral reform in the United States; and finally a bust due to the Depression, the repeal of Prohibition, and the enforcement of Mexican antigambling laws produced very irregular patterns of border crossings in the early part of this century. By 1936 traffic was at a very low point. However, this was the beginning of mutual respect and advantageous reciprocity between the nations. Ownership and control of the border enterprises was now clearly in Mexican hands. The U.S. and Mexico positions on World War II were similar, but there was still a dip in the number of U.S. tourists to Tijuana in the war years, between 1942-1945. Servicemen in San Diego and defense workers looking for rationed or scarce goods formed the bulk of the American visitors to Tijuana.

Since then the number of crossings has grown at an extremely rapid rate, rising to over six times the 1945 level. Population growth in northern Baja California and southern California, economic prosperity, relatively amiable relations between the U.S. and Mexico, the Bracero Program, and other factors all contributed to this increase.

The number of alien crossings has in the past been dependent on the number of U.S. citizen crossings, because U.S. tourism was the major support of Tijuana and Ensenada. In 1959 and 1960 the adverse publicity of certain wholesale arrests of United States citizens in Mexico led to a brief decline in tourism and is reflected in the accompanying graph on crossings. Fluctuations in U.S. tourism determined the fluctuations in the number of people employed in northern Baja California, which in turn determined the number of alien crossings. Now, with industrial and economic diversification in northern Baja California, an increase of Mexican tourism in the United States, the increase of "resident aliens" who live in Tijuana and commute for work in the United States, and other factors, there are more alien than U.S. citizen crossings,

U.S. CITIZEN BORDER CROSSINGS
1956 AND 1968, BY MONTHS—
SAN YSIDRO, CALIFORNIA

SOURCE: Unpublished data United States Immigration
Port of Entry, San Ysidro, California

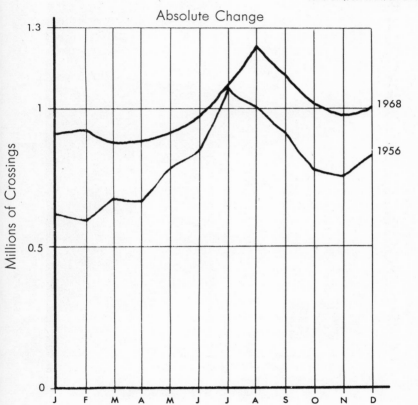

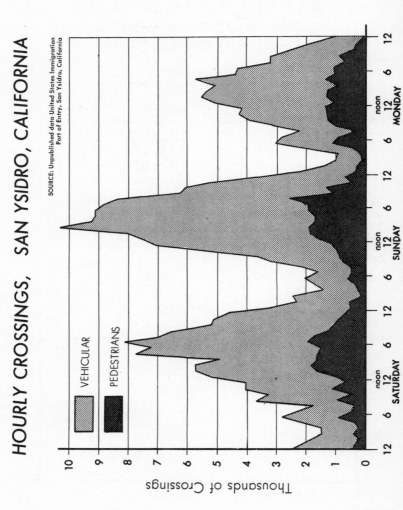

HOURLY CROSSINGS, SAN YSIDRO, CALIFORNIA

SOURCE: Unpublished data United States Immigration
Port of Entry, San Ysidro, California

and the number of alien crossings is less dependent on tourism in Mexico.

The monthly pattern of U.S. citizen crossings shows the increase of tourism in June, July, and August and the shopping for Christmas gifts in December, but this curve is flattening out somewhat over time as other business becomes more important and tourism in Mexico becomes a year-round family activity of camping, shopping, horse racing, and jai alai in Mexico. The Mexicans have still a flatter annual curve due to the importance of daily crossings for shopping and employment.

The weekly pattern is similar for aliens and U.S. citizens, except that citizens are in the majority on weekends and aliens are in the majority on weekdays. Also, Monday is more important than Saturday for aliens because of the aliens who spend the weekend in Mexico and go to work in the United States on Monday. Sunday is by far the most active day, then in turn Saturday, Monday, Friday, Thursday, Tuesday, and finally Wednesday. This order can be changed in weeks with a holiday like Thanksgiving on Thursday or Labor Day on Monday. In fact, Labor Day is usually the busiest day of the year.

The daily pattern by hours shows the most detailed, and the most extreme, fluctuations. There is the general pattern of a peak somewhere in the middle of the heavy hours of traffic from 11:00 a.m. to 8:00 p.m., and then a low point around 3:00-4:00 a.m. that has only 10-20 percent of the day's peak traffic. On weekdays there is a brief 5:00-6:00 a.m. surge of commuter workers, an 8:00 a.m. wave of school children bound for U.S. schools, then Mexican women crossing to shop in the middle of the day, and finally U.S. tourists returning in the afternoon and evening.

The peak is about 2:00 p.m. on Sundays, from 1:00-4:00 p.m. on weekdays, and 4:00-6:00 p.m. on Saturdays reflecting the impact of an earlier "Sunday-drive" traffic and a later "Saturday-night-on-the-town" traffic.

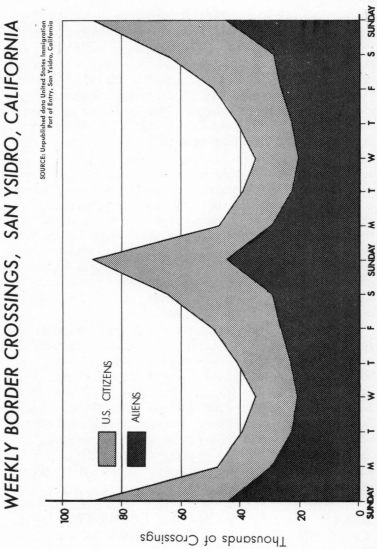

WEEKLY BORDER CROSSINGS, SAN YSIDRO, CALIFORNIA

SOURCE: Unpublished data United States Immigration
Port of Entry, San Ysidro, California

Saturday and Sunday horse racing and Sunday bullfights produce their own rush hours at the border station. The diagram on hourly crossings divides the vehicular and pedestrian traffic, showing that about three out of four persons go across in a vehicle.

iv: Contemporary Tijuana

Political Organization and Action

For most political and statistical purposes Tijuana is a *municipio*, or county, in the State of Baja California. It is 1,392 square kilometers (an area that, if square, would be about 23 miles to each side) with a *ciudad*, or central city, and three *delegaciones*, or outlying townships: La Mesa de Tijuana to the east, San Antonio de los Buenos to the south, and Rosarito farther south on the coast. The *delegaciones* have police departments, fire departments, and other government staff that are subsidiary to the municipal government, which in turn is responsive to the political party in power, the Partido Revolucionario Institucional (PRI).

There is a general division of politics between the conservative, free-enterprise, Catholic-Church aligned Partido Accion Nacional (PAN) minority and the liberal, more socialistic, somewhat anticlerical PRI majority. Businesses and voluntary organizations, except religious ones, tend to be aligned with the government and the political party structure. Also, in both party and private organizations the outside influence and resources of state and national levels are significant and occasionally dominate city politics.

Since Baja California became a state in 1953, its three governors and all its state legislators, mayors, and councilmen have been PRI members, so the March 1968 selection of candidates by PRI was seen at the time as the final choice of new officers. The opposing PAN held a vigorous campaign, and in June an estimated 240,000, or 80 percent of the voters, cast their ballots in the Baja California election. The PAN party had a very good showing in the elections and was popularly believed to have received more votes in the mayor elections in Tijuana and Mexicali. Whatever the results, the public was never told. Tabulations of the vote were delayed for several days, and finally the ballot boxes were taken to the state capitol at Mexicali without announcing the count. PAN staged a number of marches in protest, carrying signs saying "We want a new election" and a black coffin labeled "Democracy." Then the state legislature nullified the balloting for mayors in Tijuana and Mexicali on the ground that "irregularities committed . . . were of such gravity that they did not permit expressing the free will of the citizenry." The state legislature also rationalized its action by declaring that the PAN candidate in Mexicali "lacks the political capacity to be a candidate for the municipal presidency." The state governor then asked the state legislature for a constitutional amendment so that the legislature could appoint officials to run the governments of Tijuana and Mexicali instead of calling for new elections. In 1970 the PRI won the election again.

Municipal administration is carried out by an elected mayor and a municipal council, who serve a three-year term without the opportunity for reelection to successive terms. The council has a legal advisor, a treasurer, an administrative secretary, and representatives from each of the PRI sectors: rural workers, factory workers, and professional and private organizations. Except for the head of municipal tax collection all departmental heads are appointed: public security, public works, civil registration, tourism, and so forth.

Several organizations are very important in politics and city life generally. The Junta de Mejoramieto is an appointed municipal-government committee under the state director of education charged with promoting local projects of general civic welfare, such as fairs, fiestas, parades, athletic and musical programs, and so forth. This organization works in close cooperation with the PRI, the municipal administration, the Chamber of Commerce, and local service and social clubs, such as the Lions, the Masons, and the Junior Chamber of Commerce. The Groupo Feminina de Colonias is a pressure group representing the interests of the poor colonias and the poor generally. The poor colonias tend to have the most active political organizations of all the residential districts. Groupo Feminina promotes the development of such things as public works for the poor colonias, medical clinics, and adult education. Another association represents the interests of the wealthy property owners, including the major land developers. It promotes its members' interests in such matters as low property taxes, secure land titles, and the government provision of public services.

The Chamber of Commerce is the most powerful nongovernment organization, having national and international ties of importance. It has many overlapping memberships with the PRI and the government. It even has quasi-governmental functions, such as the administration of federal price controls on basic food items and monitoring compliance with business tax and license laws.

There is something of an opposed duality between the anticlerical Masons and the Catholic Church-affiliated Knights of Columbus. The latter's membership tends to be correlated with the PAN, to promote religious education and service projects, and to promote the active participation of adult males in Catholic Church programs.

Tijuana's *Directory of Social Services* lists over 100 service agencies for such things as direct relief, child care, medical and dental clinics, disability benefits, disaster services, education supporters, planned parenthood services, service clubs, youth clubs, and so forth. Tijuana has such volunteer organizations as the Junior Chamber of

Commerce, Lion's Club, Kiwanis, Rotary, Soroptimists, and the Professional Women's Club.

The labor union movement, although there are few strikes, has more vitality and political power in Mexico than in the U.S. or Canada. Labor campaigns now aim at a regular eight-hour workday and an increase in the daily minimum wage of the state. The annual May Day (Dia del Trabajo) parade and festivities are among the most important in Tijuana. Over 110 unions are represented in the parade, ranging from teachers to mariachi musicians. Soon after Dia del Trabajo there is the Cinco de Mayo parade, in which the school children march in their school uniforms to celebrate the defeat of Emperor Maxmilian's French troops at Puebla in 1862. Tijuana notes that it was once officially named after the general of the Mexican forces in that battle, Zaragosa. The parade on Cinco de Mayo in Tijuana involves over 100,000 people lining the streets to watch over 10,000 uniformed people marching by, particularly the students but also military units, policemen, and firemen. It is a confirmation of one's patriotism. The most important holiday in Tijuana, however, is still Independence Day on September 16.

Geographical Setting and Housing

Metropolitan Tijuana stretches from the coast (Playas de Tijuana) eastward along the U.S.-Mexico border for 15 miles to the Rodriguez Dam areas as follows: La Playa, three miles; La Ciudad, five miles; La Mesa, five miles; and La Presa, two miles. The Tijuana River Valley widens out northwesterly after it passes the narrow gorge at the dam to about one mile in the La Mesa area, about three miles in La Ciudad, and then flattens out into a broad coastal plain at the mouth of the valley. The border crosses the valley in such a way that all of the mouth of the valley is on the U.S. side.

The population is concentrated in the valley and in the hills and mesas adjacent to the central city. The population density in this area is greater than an area of equivalent size in San Diego. Within metropolitan Tijuana there are 131 named districts. The old heart of the city is near the border and south of the riverbed. In the old days, when water sporadically flowed, the traffic into Tijuana came across a bridge to enter the town. Now the Old Town covers all of the relatively flat land in the valley bottom southwest of the riverbed for about two miles. It is divided into three zones: 1) Zona Norte—a generally transient and lower-class residential and entertainment district for Mexicans; 2) Zona Central—the large city center that includes a) the business district along Avenida Constitution and west of that street for about three blocks, b) the center for foreign tourists along Revolucion, and c) a surrounding mixed area; and 3) Zona Este—a mixed residential and commercial district. The rest of commerce and industry in the city tends to be located along the major paved roads.

Avenida Revolucion runs south up the valley to the base of the hills and then turns southeast to become Agua Caliente Boulevard, the major highway to the east. Boulevard Reforma carries heavy traffic from the border station along the floor of the riverbed, intersects Agua Caliente Boulevard, and becomes the highway south to Ensenada. City planners hope to develop this riverbed into a modern tourist center, but today it is simply lined with dozens of automobile shops: used cars, mufflers, radiators, upholstery, junk dealers, and so on. Other major paved roads go up into the surrounding hills where the majority of the population resides. Although these roads have some commerce along them, the 128 remaining districts of the city are primarily residential.

A *colonia* is a public-supported residential district. Usually this means that the government surveys, subdivides, and grades the roads of a hillside, and then gives the lots to those who wish to build homes and reside there. At the stage when the land is free it is a *colonia popular*. Over the years as the homes are built and houses and lots are sold and resold, the district becomes simply a *colonia*. In 1968 there were no *colonia populares* and 46 *colonias* in Tijuana.

More important for Tijuana in recent years have been the *fraccionamientos*, or subdivisions, by private companies. There are 82 *fraccionamientos* in Tijuana. In some legal uses of the term, a *fraccionamiento* is a subdivision which has piped water, a sewer system, paved streets, curbs and gutters, and land set aside for a park or school. Although a few are subdivisions in the sense of tract homes built by a single construction firm, most of the *fracciona-mientos* in Tijuana do not have the above facilities and are simply a collection of house lots sold by a private owner.

The average newcomer today in the outlying poor *colonias* rents, or he may make payments on a $1,000-$1,500 lot and over time construct his own house for from $1,000-$2,000. A needed addition is a cement tank (*pila*) to hold about 1,000 liters (266 gallons) of water piped into the house, with water delivered two or three times a month. The householder builds either an outhouse or a toilet with a water flush and a cesspool. He will not have a telephone, but may have electricity. If he has a good steady income he can buy a small home and lot in an older *colonia* or an inexpensive *fraccionamiento* with a *pila* or perhaps piped city water and electricity for from $8,000-$15,000. If he is among the well-to-do he could afford a home in one of the expensive *fraccionamientos* where generally homes in the $15,000-$25,000 range are located.

Expensive residential housing is found south of Agua Caliente Boulevard on the hill slope facing the valley. The lowest class of housing, and this category includes some "squatters," or *paracaidistas*, who pay nothing for their lot, tends to be very distant from the city center in the surrounding hills and canyons or in the eastern end of the valley in La Mesa. This is where most of the six-by-nine-feet tarpaper shacks are. The 1960 data from city files in Table 4 show that Tijuana has a housing shortage, with existing facilities being small and crowded; a high percen-

TABLE 4

Tijuana Housing

No. of Rooms	Percent of Population
1	36.0%
2	27.0
3	18.3
4	9.7
5	4.0
6 or more	5.0

Average persons per room 2.4

Average rooms per house 2.3

Renters	61%	
Houses with water service	57%	
Houses with sewer service	37%	
Houses with electric service (1968)	47,700	89.0%

tage of renters; and inadequate publicly operated water and sewer services.

The city is laid out in a patchwork of grid patterns that run perpendicular and parallel to the major streets. Thus, instead of flowing along the contours of a hill, streets charge straight up even extremely steep hills. Since most of the streets are not paved, the erosion on the steep streets is very severe. Of the 131 districts in Tijuana only three new, exclusive *fraccionamientos* have contoured streets. The Chamber of Commerce (1968: 6-7) reports that 21 percent of the city streets are paved. Paving, cement curbs and gutters, and sidewalks are essentially limited to the downtown zones, the major boulevards of the city, and some exclusive *fraccionamientos*. Garbage collecting is also limited to these parts of the city, while most people burn their garbage or load it in the back of the car and dump it somewhere, usually in the valley floor near the riverbed.

Colonia Libertad is the largest district in the city and, with a beginning in the late 1920s, the oldest primarily residential district. It is northeast of the riverbed with an estimated 1968 population of 35,000, or some 11 percent of the total population. In Table 5 are compared our Libertad findings with Mexico City data, and a survey of 100 households in Tecate, a city 33 miles east of Tijuana. The prosperity of Tijuana and Tecate in the private sector is evident in such terms as high household incomes and high levels of ownership of vehicles, television receivers, and other appliances. However, prosperity has had much less impact in the public sector of utilities such as piped water, sewer drainage, and the paving and lighting of residential streets (Price, 1967 and 1968; Banco de Londres y Mexico, 1967).

TABLE 5

Income, Housing, and the Household Possession of Appliances in Tijuana, Tecate, and Mexico City

	Libertad, Tijuana (1968)	Tecate (1967)	Mexico City (1960)
Monthly household income	$225	$229	$171
Housing			
Occupant is proprietor	51%	65%	21%
1 or 2 rooms	63%	19%	66%
Piped water	8%	57%	89%
Sewer drainage	60%	42%	55%
Appliances			
Radio	78%	83%	85%
Television	75%	69%	30%
Gas stove	72%	81%	
Refrigerator	57%	69%	
Washing machine	49%	60%	

Urban Facilities

Water and Sewer System

Water pollution and inadequate quantities of water have been chronic problems for Tijuana. Without a sewer system in most of the city the underground water is too polluted to be potable. The water from Rodriguez Dam and from city-owned wells that flow through the city water system is heavily chlorinated and is usually medically satisfactory for human consumption, but it carries a heavy load of brown sediment and is irregular in flow. My 1968 field station in downtown Tijuana had water available, but usually only for an hour or two a day, from 4:30 to 6:30 in the morning. If we did not get up at dawn to take a shower, we missed a shower that day. Except for a few outlying wells people generally do not drink either the tap water or the well water.

The consumption of bottled drinks takes an inordinately large part of the family budget, especially in Tijuana, although drinking beer and carbonated beverages seems to be a national cultural trait. Part of the rationale for drinking bottled beverages is that they are medicinally pure, but this practice carries over to towns like Tecate where the water supply is pure. In fact, water drawn in Tecate is sold for consumption in Tijuana.

There are ten water-bottling plants in Tijuana that sell an estimated 38,000 gallons per day of either imported water or purified well water. Collectively they distribute about 8,000 bottles a day, each bottle containing five gallons and costing $1.17 on the retail market. Water for the *pila* storage tanks is supplied by seven water-delivery companies, the largest of which has 25 trucks. Each tanker truck holds 1,000 gallons, and the charge for one truckload is $2. The cost is primarily for hauling the water, because a tanker full of water at the pump is only 30 cents. The current underground water level in the riverbed is about 225 feet from the surface at the pumps near the border, although the water comes to the surface to form a pond farther up the valley at Agua Caliente.

The average sources of water for Tijuana are 350 liters per second from Rodriguez Dam, 150 liters per second from the Tijuana riverbed, and 200 liters per second from La Mision, for a total of 700 liters per second supplied by current sources. The minimum need for water in 1978 is estimated at 1,600 liters per second, 900 liters more than the current sources. In order to help meet this demand the Mexican government has just completed construction of the world's largest desalination plant, next to the Rosarito power station. The local public water corporation has a contract with the Federal Power Commission to purchase 329 liters per second (7.5 million gallons per day) from the desalination plant for the next 20 years. This relatively expensive (17 cents a ton) additional source of supply will still be inadequate to meet the needs of Tijuana in 1978.

Tijuana is currently carrying out a $16 million program to install a complete water purification and pipe distribution system in the city. It is also working on a $10 million sewer system that will provide proper drainage for the city. The city will have a continuous need for more agricultural and industrial water, but at least the domestic water supply will be pure and consistently available in a pipe system. The current water pipe system covers essentially the old downtown area, some of the adjacent *colonias*, and has an extension that includes several of the expensive *colonias* and *fraccionamientos* to the south of Agua Caliente. There is a great disparity between the volume of water used between those who have access to piped water (216 liters per day) and those who lack this access (18 liters per day).

Transportation

No one knows how many of the people of Tijuana own cars because a significant proportion of the residents do not register their cars in Mexico or buy Mexican license plates. Based on counts of license plates, about 40 percent of the cars of residents of Tijuana have California license plates. Of these California plates 32 percent were out of date, mostly for cars brought from the U.S. but not used for driving in the U.S. All Mexican citizen-residents are legally supposed to register their cars and to buy plates, but the cost is high at $60-$70. An estimate by the Departmento Transito plus the correction for California plates indicates that about 75 percent of the households have one or more vehicles. Tijuana probably has the highest per capita ownership of cars in Mexico. In 1965 only about 10 percent of the households in all of Mexico owned cars. Tijuana also has an extensive bus service that provides service to the most distant *colonias.*

Communication

Communication facilities are fairly adequate. Tijuana has five daily newspapers and such quality magazines as *Chronica Social de Baja California* for social coverage and *Baja California Magazine* for general coverage. The latter is among the forces that is currently promoting the conversion of Avenida Revolucion into a modern shopping mall. Eleven radio and two television stations broadcast from Tijuana, but some of these are English-language stations beamed for Southern California from Mexico because the operation of the station is less expensive in Mexico. Television station XEWT broadcasts in Spanish and XETV (an American Broadcasting Corporation station) broadcasts in English. The city has 12,500 telephones, of which 5,700 (45.6 percent) are residential, about 11 percent of the residences having telephones. There are very few public telephones, so that it is common to have to wait in a long line to use one. Mail service tends to be the most inadequate of the communication facilities with slow and often incorrect delivery and extremely few mailboxes or post offices. Because some 19 percent of the adult Tijuanese do not read or write, Tijuana has a number of public scribes, especially in the area of the post office.

Medical Care

Medical facilities are fairly good for a Mexican city of 385,000. In 1968 Tijuana had 4 hospitals, 11 clinics, 7 sanitariums, 193 medical doctors, 69 dentists, and 16 optical shops. The social security program of Mexico emphasizes health insurance and provides special social security hospitals, so that many families with low incomes still have adequate medical care. The medical facilities of Tijuana are also used by U.S. citizens, particularly Mexican-Americans, primarily because equivalent services cost 30-40 percent less than in the U.S. Tijuana has some cancer clinics that use drugs legally banned in the U.S.—such as laetrile (ground apricot pits), Krebiozen, and glyoxylide—and thus attract some cancer patients who have tried unsuccessfully to cure their cancer with other drugs. Some Mexican doctors will perform illegal abortions (about $300 for a competent doctor), but Baja California has become increasingly strict concerning abortions, while California has become more lenient. For example, Baja California's state penal code now prohibits bail for persons charged with performing an abortion or submitting to such an operation.

Education

The education system seems to be inadequate in both facilities and staff. Brenton (1963: 68) reported on 52 primary schools, of which 44 were public schools that had only 477 teachers for 21,000 pupils, a high teacher-student ratio of 1:44. There were also 10 secondary schools with 2,061 students, but there was an extremely high dropout rate after the sixth grade. In Baja California's public schools as a whole in 1969 the classrooms averaged between 40 and 50 students, and most schools had two or three sessions a day. Extensive school construction is underway in a program in which the federal government finances 50 percent, the state finances 25 percent, and the community provides the final 25 percent, primarily from voluntary donations. The Universidad Autonoma de Baja California has its School of Commerce and Administration in Tijuana.

In related service a free public sports complex was built on the federally owned banks of the Tijuana River. It includes a soccer stadium that will hold 6,000 people, a baseball field, and courts for basketball, handball, and tennis. It also has an auditorium, a gymnasium, and a swimming pool.

Economics

It is difficult to collect accurate data on commerce and industry in Tijuana, because a high proportion of the enterprises are extremely small operations that do not register with the Chambers of Commerce or Industry. The manufacture of goods for sale to tourists typically takes place in shops that are within or attached to private homes by the family members. Paper and plastic flowers, velvet paintings, leather goods, and piñatas are typically made in private homes, while wrought-iron works, plaster statuary, and glassware are made in larger shops. Although produced in large quantities for a mass market, the small-scale operations, hand crafting, and competition among producers have led to some excellent workmanship and creativity in even mundane media such as papier-mâché piñatas. Connoisseurs of Mexican folk art also find that, in addition to a lot of mediocrity, fine art pieces from all parts of Mexico are brought in for sale in Tijuana. Four interesting local tourist crafts are plaster statuary, glass blowing, painting on velvet, and piñatas.

There are several plaster statuary shops on the hill east of the border station. These shops produce some 200 kinds of statues that sell from 50 cents to $3. The items are mostly pedestals, urns, busts, animals, and relief carvings. A specialist makes the molds of about twelve layers of liquid latex. The latex molds are supported by an exterior plaster foundation and then filled over and over with casting plaster that sets in twenty minutes. The white statuary is usually painted with a leathery-looking antique brown pigment made by mixing wax and gasoline. A medium-sized shop turns out some 100 pieces a day, at a cost of about 20 cents each, which are sold in small wholesale lots for final retail sale at an average of $1 each.

The glass works on Avenida Revolucion in Tijuana was such a tourist attraction that it put in rows of seats, a soft-drink machine, and a receptacle where specific glass-blowers can be tipped by tourists for their spectacular performances. A "Venetian glass" process is used, employing thick glass with flecks, swirls, and pieces of brightly colored glass in the final pieces. The main furnace usually contains a large pool of slightly tinted glass. Then in this pool they float three or four pots that each contain a different color of molten glass. The blower first picks up a glob of glass at the end of his metal blowing pipe which he then blows and shapes. Then he adds other colors and parts, making many elaborate forms, especially vases or statues. Clowns and animals are popular forms. The pieces are placed in a tempering oven for 72 hours, and then rough spots or spurs are filed off.

The Tijuana factory employs several blowers, each with an apprentice. Each blower makes from 20 to 40 pieces a day, depending on their elaborateness. Most of the glass-blowers come from Guadalajara or Juarez, although a few are in apprenticeship at the factory. It takes about five years for an apprentice to become a skilled glassblower. Once known in the profession, these men make good wages and travel quite a bit, usually staying at one place for only several months. This movement seems to be related to the fact that the various blowers have specialized in several kinds of pieces that they do well, so they travel from one shop to the next doing their speciality work. All the blowers seem to know how to make drinking glasses and vases, but skills related to making the various kinds of elaborate glass statuary are more esoteric.

Paintings on velvet are designs copied from other paintings and magazines that are reproduced by the hundreds. A stencil is made by sketching on a large piece of paper and then punching small holes with a nail along the lines of the drawing. The drawing is then repeatedly placed on black velvet and brushed with powdered chalk to leave outlines for the painter. Bright acrylic paints are then used for painting in what is usually a single large figure, leaving the surrounding black velvet for contrast. The subjects are mostly tigers or other wild animals, costumed natives, land or seascapes, wide-eyed children, and nudes. Most of the artists work in their homes and produce from one to five paintings a day, depending on the size of painting and the care that they take. Even beginning painters can sell their wares if they are priced low enough because so many tourists come looking for bargain souvenirs. It takes about a year of work for the average artist to bring his earnings up to $20 a day.

Piñatas are papier-mâché forms that are filled with candies, peanuts in the shell, cookies, and occasionally small toys and fruit. At parties on Christmas, birthdays, and a person's saint's name day the adults swing the *piñata* on a rope while the children take turns trying to break it open by hitting it with a bat while they are blindfolded. When the *piñata* is broken, the fillings fall to the floor, and the children scramble for them. The traditional form had a thin clay pot in the center, but these are no longer made because people think they are too expensive. The artists make any form that they think will amuse children: funny animals, clowns, Santas, Batman, and so on.

Piñatas are often made in homes, especially around Christmas. A clay pot is usually used as a form to make the central papier-mâché shell of old newspapers, pasted with a flour-and-water glue. Protruding parts are then built out of the central shell with bailing wire and more newspapers. Finally, the form is covered with several sheets of colored tissue paper, often cut so that it is fringed. A skilled artisan can produce about two $2 *piñatas* per hour.

Even more than manufacturing, the retailing and services are predominantly small operations. Tijuana has several professional beggars. Children sell gum or newspapers, shine shoes, and clean cars while street vendors with carts sell such snack foods as ice cream, steamed tacos, fruit, soft drinks, and steamed corn on the cob. Some vendors simply buy a case of the fruit that is in season and then carry the case around and ask people to buy some. These itinerant vendors are persistent, high-pressure salesmen, among Mexicans as well as with tourists. Selling from pushcarts was outlawed along the main tourist street because they blocked pedestrian traffic, but men still sell watches and jewelry from small, open display cases that they carry suspended from their necks. Around Guerrero Park and other places where large numbers of Mexicans park their cars men elicit jobs of waxing or fixing the dents of cars.

Another feature that confuses the economic picture of Tijuana is the high economic integration of Tijuana with the U.S. There are over 8,000 Mexicans with "permanent residence alien" visas ("green cards") to immigrate into the U.S. who, instead of immigrating, continue to reside in Tijuana and, in effect, use the card as a permit to work in the U.S. They thus serve as a population that is a solid link between U.S. and Mexican culture, and they contribute very heavily to the economy of Tijuana. There is some question about the proportion of their income that they spend in Tijuana, but their per capita contribution is certainly very great. With an average household size of about six, they give direct support to some 50,000 people. The "multiplier effect" of spending and respending of this income within the community is very important for the employment of additional persons, because high U.S. wages are being spent in an area with low wages. A multiplier of two would be a conservative estimate, so that indirectly the more than 8,000 employed in the U.S. would purchase goods and services in Tijuana and thus support about 8,000 additional workers and their families for a total support of some 100,000 people. The average green-card worker thus provides support directly or indirectly for about 12 Tijuanese. This process has a lot to do with why Tijuana has grown so rapidly and why, for example, Juarez (500,000 population) is now larger than its sister city in the U.S., El Paso (300,000 population). At about $100 a week income for these green-card workers, collectively they would earn some $43 million a year.

In 1967 some 52 percent of the estimated 23,605,469 people who entered the U.S. from Tijuana were aliens, and about 99 percent of those aliens were Mexicans. About 34,000 inhabitants of Tijuana entered the U.S. every day. Put another way, over 10 percent of the Tijuanese entered the U.S. daily. The major reasons why Mexicans enter the U.S. are economic in character, for either work or shopping in the U.S. About 26,000 aliens enter the U.S. on "border-crossing cards" ("blue cards," issued to permanent residents of Mexico who live near the border, allow a 72-hour visit within 25 miles of the border and are not working permits) and a few tourist (six months, no areal limit) or other kinds of visas. Perhaps as many as two or three thousand of these blue-card workers have jobs in the U.S. I have talked to dozens of maids, cooks, cleaning men, agricultural workers, and others who hold only blue cards and work in the San Diego area. Certainly they too make some contribution to the income of Tijuana.

Mexican-Americans who are U.S. citizens are consistent and sophisticated shoppers in Tijuana. They speak the language and they know where to go and what to buy at prices that are cheaper than in the U.S. While haircuts are $2-3 in San Diego, they are only $1 in Tijuana. The services of beauty parlors, photographers, dressmakers and tailors, automobile mechanics, and many other labor-intensive services are 50-60 percent cheaper in Tijuana than in San Diego. Tijuana has a large Mexican-American population to attract, with some 2 million Spanish-surname people in California.

Most of the average dollar spent by a tourist in Tijuana

is eventually respent by Mexicans in Southern California. Housewives cross the border to buy chickens, lard, beans, rice, eggs, potatoes, and other food items that are less expensive in the U.S. Mexican retailers and wholesalers purchase heavily in the U.S., in part simply because of the relative inaccessibility and long transport haul from the markets of interior Mexico.

Industries that are not dependent on the tourist trade are beginning to play a role in the economy of Tijuana. Cigarettes, paints, iron and steel goods, and clothing are made from basic materials in Tijuana, and the city has "dual-plant" assembly plants for clothing and electronic parts sent from the U.S. Warwick Electronics of Illinois employs over 500 workers in its Tijuana factory (Electronica de Baja California) which manufactures television receivers for Sears, Roebuck & Co. Electronica's basic wage for assemblers is 45 pesos ($3.60) per day. The majority of commerce in Tijuana is concerned with 1) tourist goods (both imported and of local manufacture), 2) family entertainment (horse racing, bullfights, and *jai alai*), and 3) ordinary services (beauticians, barbers, doctors, dentists, car upholstery, and so on). The Tijuana Chamber of Commerce estimated that foreign visitors spent $60 million in 1967 in the city (while the San Diego Chamber of Commerce estimated that Mexicans spent $76.7 million in San Diego County in the same year).

Several factors continue to promote Tijuana's tourist-based economy. Tijuana, along with Ensenada, Tecate, and Mexicali, is within the border zone of Mexico that allows free entry without a visa or tourist card. Also important are its free-port status, easy access for military personnel stationed in the San Diego area 18 miles away, and the easy access generally between Tijuana and the industrial and urban portions of Southern California with its 14 million people.

The importance of tourism to the economy of Tijuana sometimes hides the fact that it is a city with a large internal commerce and industry. The diversity of this

Sheilah Graham and F. Scott Fitzgerald were among the many Hollywood notables to grace the Tijuana scene in the early days.

Culver Pictures, Inc.

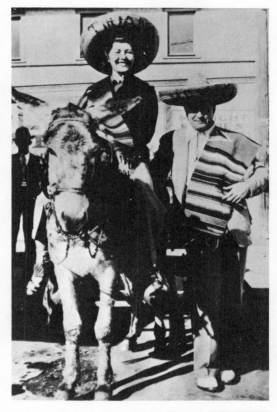

Aqua Caliente, the site of natural hot springs in Tijuana, became a world-famous spa and gambling casino between 1926 and 1935.

Culver Pictures, Inc.

The Tijuana-San Ysidro port-of-entry is one of the world's busiest, now handling over 30 million crossings each year.

Avenida Revolucion is a mile-long strip of bars, restaurants, and shops selling tourist goods.

Arcades along Revolucion are filled with small shops and an occasional guitar or marimba band.

Fine crafts from all over Mexico are sold in the arcades of Revolucion, but two-dollar plaster statuary is the best selling item.

Zona Norte is a district of transient residence, country-style entertainment with mariachi bands, and prostitution.

Tropical and subtropical fruits and vegetables fill the grocery stores while few canned and highly processed foods are sold.

internal commerce is illustrated in the lists of over 10,000 businesses registered with the electric service, the telephone company, or the Chambers of Commerce and Industry. For example, in the automotive field there are 287 businesses: 106 in used cars, 78 gas stations, 42 in car parts, 23 in car repair, 15 in upholstery, 12 in tires, 10 in commercial transport, and 1 new car dealer.

Revolucion: The Tourist Street

Other than horse racing and bullfighting, most of the foreign tourist facilities in Tijuana are concentrated along Avenida Revolucion from First to Eighth Street. Generally the quality of the bars, curio shops, clothing stores, and so forth improves as you go up the street. Thus, tourists usually enter the street at the bottom, closest to the border-crossing point, where there are several striptease and go-go girl bars. Tourists usually pass these by for the more than 200 shops selling Mexican crafts and the restaurants. The Palacio Fronton, where the *jai alai* games are played, is at the top of the avenue on Eighth Street. Glass-blowing demonstrations and sales of blown glass are also on the avenue across from the Fronton.

The sidewalks are narrow and crowded with tourists, vendors, men calling people into the bars, and shoeshine boys. We found that many Mexicans stroll the street to visit their friends who work there or just to watch the tourists. Vendors try to sell you a "gold" watch or a "diamond" ring from small cases they carry. At the intersections there are usually three or four taxi drivers soliciting trade. They ask to take you back to the border, the racetrack, to some girls, or to see some dirty movies. "What are guys looking for? Girls? Pills? Hop in my cab and I'll take you." At some corners there is a donkey cart where you can sit down and have a souvenir photograph taken of yourself wearing a wide sombrero.

Most of the stores along the street sell a wide variety of Mexican crafts: serapes, tire-soled sandals, sombreros, guitars, plaster statuary, paintings on velvet, plastic flowers, chess sets and so on. We counted 126 of these "standard tourist goods" shops along the avenue in 1968. In addition, there were 76 specialty shops concentrating on such things as jewelry, liquor, leather goods, wrought iron, and pottery. Some of the shops are along arcades, especially between Third and Fourth Streets, which go back into the block. Avenida Revolucion also has dozens of service shops such as barbers, beauty parlors, shoeshine stands, doctors, lawyers, and marriage and divorce agencies.

The character of the street shifts sharply as evening comes on. In the day there are more family groups, including many women who just bring their children down for the day to do some shopping. They often come to save money on silver jewelry, imported crystal or china, or custom-made furniture. Many have learned that you can bargain with the shopkeepers on price. Later on in the evening there is more of a young male crowd of servicemen and university students and couples who come to the bars and to stroll the streets. Some of the tourist goods shops stay open as late as 2:00 or 3:00 a.m. on summer weekends to catch this late crowd, but most close around 9:00 or 10:00 p.m. A few of the bars are open all night for two or three nights a week, essentially as long as there are customers. However, not many tourists stay in Tijuana, because the hotel and motel facilities are so poor, so most are on their way back to the U.S. by midnight.

Taxi drivers in Tijuana rent their cabs for $4 for the twelve day hours or $5 for the twelve night hours. They pay the rent once a week and keep the rest of their gross earnings, which means that they net about $50 per week if they hustle. It is a very competitive business. When a taxi driver takes a group to a brothel he will usually receive a dollar per customer from the brothel and then just wait a half-hour or so and receive a return fare from the group.

The street-corner photographers are better organized. They keep their carts parked in the same lot and post only one cart per intersection. They retain their same locations day after day, and all charge $1 per picture. With some effort at selling they can then make between $10 and $20 a day.

Shoeshine stands are limited in number and permission for their locations are handed out as political favors by the local government. The men operating these pay their union 50 cents a week and the municipal government $6 per year for the privilege of working on the street. Shoeshine boys without permits are arrested if they are caught working on Avenida Revolucion. Even casual, itinerant sidewalk merchants, such as vendors of jewelry or men selling wrought ironware out of their car trunks, are controlled on Revolucion. They pay at least $10 per month to the muncipal government for the privilege of selling on the street. The government, on the other hand, is tolerant of minor frauds by the sellers, such as claiming that a watch is an expensive make.

Based on traffic counts and projections, about 5 million of the 11 million annual tourists to Tijuana visit Revolucion each year. This is comparable to such major tourist attractions as Disneyland, Yellowstone National Park, and Niagara Falls. Tijuana has become one of the important tourist attractions in North America. Because of the concentration of tourist facilities along Revolucion, activities along the street are heavily policed, licensed, and taxed. The Mexicans operating along the street form an intensive social environment of salesmen, restauranters, night club workers, taxi drivers, policemen, and so forth.

The Mexicans know each other, watch each other, and form an integrated system of social networks into which the tourist enters as a resource, the ultimate reason for the presence of the Mexicans on the street. Thus there developed a code of cooperation among the Mexicans to give special considerations, services, and kindnesses to tourists on the street. For example, there is virtually no theft, pickpocketing, soliciting by streetwalking prostitutes, mugging, or other crimes by Mexicans against tourists, except some minor frauds in merchandise claims. The stable social network moves very quickly against the entrance of un-authorized, unlicensed Mexicans generally, but clamps down extremely hard on crimes against tourists. Campaign promises of candidates for mayor of Tijuana invariably center on how they will improve Tijuana's reputation and expand tourist facilities.

Thus, Revolucion has recently acquired an excellent reputation among tens of millions of regular tourist visitors as a safe place to shop and have fun. Most of the crimes along the street are petty ones by the tourists themselves, such as "drunk and disorderly behavior" and "disrespect for a police officer." When a bar gets out of line, the local newspapers do not hesitate to attack it and force the police through public awareness to close it down, even though the police may receive graft payments from the club. The newspapers may attack a club as "a true center of vice and depravity, inviting presentations of immoral acts between the women who work there and their clients." This kind of behavior was quietly ignored in earlier years.

Prostitution

There are no laws against prostitution in Tijuana. There is a federal law, however, against the procurer or pimp who works as the liaison between the customer and the prostitute. The growth of the American family tourism, the relative decline in the number of young servicemen in Tijuana's tourist trade, the expansion of other forms of female employment, and moralistic pressures from the Tijuanese themselves have greatly reduced the amount of prostitution in Tijuana since the "wild 1940s" and forced the girls who do solicit off the streets and into certain bars, hotels, and private homes. Taxi drivers sometimes act as procurers for specific girls, but more often they take the customers to a particular bar in Zona Norte which employs girls who serve as prostitutes in addition to their jobs as bar girls and dancers. Along with a few private homes in

Zona Norte, this place also shows lewd movies where prostitutes come in and caress the male viewers to set up contracts.

The prostitution business is high pressured and blatantly commercial. The customer typically makes a contract for about $5 only to find that there are additional itemized charges "for the use of the room," "the use of the bed," and so on that bring the total to about $15. There are guards to insure that the customer pays his bill. One man told me his wallet was stolen by the girl without his being aware of it. A young serviceman said that some guards at the house went through his clothes and shoes for more money. In a third case a man paid the girl before the act only to have her leave the bar through a back door.

This high-pressure situation and the thefts could be eased if enough customers would find a Mexican lawyer and file criminal complaints against such actions. However, most customers are convinced that they have engaged in an illegal act and are not willing to take the chance of their own arrest. It is against U.S. military law for military personnel to enter known houses of prostitution. Also the U.S. military today maintains a "low profile" in Mexico by refusing to allow U.S. military personnel to wear their uniforms while on leave visits to Mexico and by refusing to give out information about the number of leave visits or arrests of U.S. military personnel in Mexico.

Almost all of the approximately 75 girls who work as bar girls and dancers along Avenida Revolucion are said to prostitute themselves regularly, and a moderate percentage of the girls who work in the dime-a-dance bars that cater to Mexicans are prostitutes. There are clearly more girls who cater to the Mexican clientele than girls who cater to foreigners, but those who cater to the Mexican clientele have fewer contracts per girl per month. A few hundred prostitutes are checked every week at the public health clinic in Tijuana according to a regular schedule, so that all girls who operate out of a specific bar come in on the same day of the week. By the definition of a prostitute as a girl who has one or more prostitution contracts per month there are approximately 1,000 prostitutes in Tijuana: 200 with a primarily foreign clientele, 100 with a mixed clientele, and 700 with a primarily Mexican clientele.

Juarez, a Mexican border city with a population of about 500,000 is larger than Tijuana, but Tijuana has a greater volume of tourist traffic than Juarez. In 1969 Juarez had 1,024 registered prostitutes with a median age of 28, only 9.4 percent of whom were born locally in Juarez, and they had an average of 2.3 living children (McNamara, 1971).

Prostitution is one of the highest paying forms of employment in Tijuana. Depending on their clientele and the number of contracts per month these girls earn, assuming averages of a net income of $5 per contract and 30 contracts per month, about $150 a month in prostitution and an additional $60 a month from the sale of drinks as bar girls or from dime-a-dance receipts. In Juarez in 1960 $60 a month was considered a good income for prostitutes (Christian, 1961: 54). In the social relations with true prostitutes selection of partners is rather indiscriminate, each maintains a fictitious personality, the relationship is usually brief, and the manner of payment emphasizes the material rather than affection ends involved. Prostitution is thus characterized by impersonality and emotional indifference or mutual contempt, and it thrives in places like border cities where language and cultural differences foster impersonality and contempt between the adjacent societies.

Colonia Libertad

Two students, Roberta Jacobs and Marianne Gerson, lived for a month in the typical residential district of Colonia Libertad. They (Price 1968 A:5:2) studied 37 families in their neighborhood. The average length of residency in Tijuana of these families was 13 years. They had moved to Libertad because the lots and houses were cheap, relatives or their work was nearby, or they enjoyed the greater space and peacefulness of the area. In the 1920s it was mostly brushland with only 300 families living there. One informant said that he had been given a parcel of land in Libertad as part of his salary, but it was of so little value at the time that he lost it in a poker game. In the 1930s many substantial houses were built in Libertad close to the city. Then, in the mid-1940s, in government-supported land development, house lots farther up on the hill were essentially given away for $10 to individuals who would build houses and reside on the lots. Today these lots sell for about $1,200.

Although the terrain of Libertad is very hilly, a grid pattern of streets was laid out. It has 11 wide streets that were bulldozed vertically up the main hill, and then smaller streets were laid out perpendicularly to these. Only a few main streets are paved, so that heavy erosion results when it rains and dust fills the air when it is dry.

Life today in Libertad focuses on Libertad rather than on downtown Tijuana. One man in the neighborhood sample played the guitar at a restaurant in the tourist area and another did paintings on velvet that were sold there, but central Tijuana is rarely visited and then mostly for such things as the post office, a doctor, or to go to the movies. However, Libertad is close to the border-crossing station, so that three men in the sample worked as inspectors there and five men worked in the U.S.: one as a baker in San Diego, two as construction workers, and two as agricultural field workers. The close proximity of the border station also means that many of the residents of Libertad regularly buy things in the U.S. that are cheaper, such as chickens, lard, beans, rice, and milk. Two-thirds of the neighborhood sample shopped for food in the U.S., usually about once a week. The 30 percent of the sample who did not shop in the U.S. said the reason was that they did not have border-crossing cards to enter the U.S.

It takes a lot of hustling to get by in Tijuana. Men often have secondary jobs, as a part-time salesman, or janitor, or mechanic, and so on. Wives and older children often work. Extended families often share the same house. They usually cannot afford to have piped-in drinking water, and normally have an outdoor toilet or a flush system from a private water tank to a septic tank. The usual lack of paving or lighting in the public streets is seen by most residents as important problems. People come to Tijuana to partake of its relative affluence, with high pay and much more material wealth, but they find a very high cost of living and many difficulties in daily living. Urban neighborhoods, such as the one studied in Libertad, seem to have even less friendliness and sociability than would be found in U.S. and Canadian cities. People usually find their significant social ties outside their neighborhood. There are often personal networks of relatives and fellow workers (*compañeros de trabajo*) that involve much socializing; however, the pressure to hustle just to survive is strong, and people say they have very little time for social activities. They work, they raise their families, they go to church, and there just is not much time left over. They say that the really bright future of prosperity in Tijuana belongs to their children.

Religion

Tijuana is neither the agnostic, hedonistic, rough border town as imaged by many casual visitors to Avenida Revolucion nor is it the Church-dominated peasant community of traditional Mexican ethnographies. Nominally almost everyone is affiliated with a Christian church, about 90 percent as Catholics. However, among Catholics religion tends to be social, conventional, and external rather than an active and emotional religiosity. The priests have a difficult time bringing the deeper meanings of the Mass and catechism to the people. Theology does not permeate daily life. Only about one-fourth of the Catholic people attend church services regularly and only about one percent regularly receive the church sacraments. Few people ever go to confession. Free-union marriages are common and carry little stigma.

Of those who do go to church, over two-thirds are women. Even when men go to church, they often do so to escort their wives and children and leave after a few minutes to congregate with other men outside. Religion is seen as something for women and children, who should pray, remain pure, and attend church. Catholic schools are seen as appropriate for children, particularly girls, but most people cannot afford the tuition for these private schools. The identity of Catholics with their church is very strong, even if they do not attend services. However, there is little antagonism toward the Protestants. They are small in numbers. They present no social threat since they tend to be poorer, more recently arrived, and more alienated from general city life. Catholics generally feel that people who leave the Catholic Church to become Protestants do so for materialistic reasons, particularly the free food and clothing given by missionaries after the services.

Protestants themselves find a vitalizing social, intellectual, and emotional life in their churches. The Protestant congregations are small, personalistic, and socially very active, with Sunday schools for children and dances for adolescents. Intensive Bible study and comparison of Catholic and Protestant practices sharpens the intellectual approach to religion among even lay church members. The Catholic Church is condemned for distorting the Bible, the worship of idols, papal infallibility, birth control, clerical celibacy, and the separation of people from God through priestcraft and ritual. For Protestants the church becomes the dominant institution in ther lives, while for Catholics the religious institution tends to play a more minor role along with kinship, occupational, and other institutions.

v: The Drug Traffic of Tijuana

A drug-using subculture of considerable magnitude developed in the U.S. in the 1960s. Initially the major increase in the use of drugs was simply around such new pharmaceuticals as barbiturates, amphetamines, and LSD. These were acquired from sources within the U.S., so their flow never presented a problem for international relations. The search for new drug experiences, however, soon led to an increased use of older, "natural" drugs with sources outside the U.S.: marijuana, opium, cocaine, peyote, and psychedelic mushrooms. These were drawn from particular areas of the world, creating some stress in international relations between the U.S. and those source areas.

Marijuana is simply the hemp plant that was originally domesticated for its fibers in South Asia. Technically, it is *Cannibus sativa*, but as a drug plant in Mexico it was called *marijuana*, "Mary Jane," or *Mota*. When the U.S. was cut off from Asian supplies of hemp during World War II, the crop was greatly expanded in Mexico. Mexico became a major producer of industrial hemp and thus shifted easily into concentrating production on the more resinous female plant when its use as a drug plant became popular in the U.S. Roughly 80 percent of the marijuana and 20 percent of the heroin used in the U.S. comes from Mexico. Estimates of Mexican marijuana in the U.S. range around 300 tons per year.

89778

Under initial pressures from the U.S. and more recent fears of the spread of a drug culture within Mexico, the Mexican police and army began destroying the marijuana crops and opium poppy fields. Every year for the last few years the Mexican Army has destroyed over 3,000 small fields of illegal drug crops. This forced a shift of much of the drug farming into small, inaccessible mountainous farms in the Sierra Madre Occidental. In order of their importance in 1969, estimates of their contribution to the total drug crop for the major producing states are Jalisco, 38 percent; Sinaloa, 26 percent; Michoacan, 17 percent; and Durango, 15 percent.

Several years ago dealers (*marijuanos*) delivered only to the border towns where they would resell in large quantities to U.S. wholesalers and to Mexicans who would retail by the kilogram brick. Now dealers will deliver anywhere in the U.S. However, more important are the U.S. wholesalers, many of them Mexican-Americans, who drive to the interior towns and make their own deals with 1) jobbers who buy up blocks of marijuana in the field and process it or with 2) the entrepreneurs who finance the operations of dozens of small farmers.

So that they cannot be spotted from the air, the fields are kept down to only one-third to one-half of an acre and the marijuana plants may be mixed with corn plants. An acre produces about 5,000 plants, which provides about one ton of marijuana. A field that is well watered and fertilized will produce two or even three crops per year. Each plant is harvested individually as it blossoms. The farmer checks the resin content by squeezing the flowering tops. If the resin is sticky it is ready to harvest. The branches are separated from the main stalks and allowed to dry for about one week, while the flowering "tops" are trimmed off and sold separately for about twice as much as the leaves. The stems are then screened out, and the leaves are mixed with a packing agent, usually made of sugar and water. Connoisseurs are particularly critical about the amount of stems and sugar in the marijuana. Also there is some salesmanship and promotion of one area's marijuana over that from another area. Acapulco Gold, Zacatecas Purple, and Panama Gold are romantic names that are supposed to refer to where the marijuana is raised, while the color of the plant is always the same. It is, of course, raised, not in Acapulco or Panama, but in Jalisco and other west-central areas. The buyers smoke samples to test the plants very carefully and sit around comparing them to other marijuana they have tried. They also talk about bribery payments and methods of smuggling (Tichbone, 1970).

A hydraulic jack or some other makeshift press is used to force the marijuana into a brick form that usually ranges from about 28 to 30 ounces in weight. This is called a "kilogram," "kilo," "key," or "brick." A true kilogram is 35.27 ounces, so these "kilos" tend to be a little light. After being pressed into the shape of a brick, the marijuana is packaged in brown wrapping paper and sealed with tape. Some have even been stamped with "trademarks."

The farmer can sell a ton of plants at the farm site for about $3,500. One ton of dried, cleaned, and packaged marijuana can be delivered for about $20,000 in a city in west-central Mexico or delivered to a city in the Southwest U.S. for about $30,000. When these bulk quantities are involved, smuggling over the border costs less than one-third of the price, but the value of the goods increases steadily because of the danger in simply handling the goods, particularly in the U.S.

In the U.S. the ton lots are sold by kilos, for from about $100 to $200 per kilo depending on the quality of the goods and current market conditions. Small retail dealers in turn break a kilo down into one-ounce lots called "lids" (from the old tin tobacco cans that had hinged lids) or "baggies." Today the ounce lots are usually sold in small plastic bags for about $15 each.

For a single kilo the Mexican farmer receives about $3, the Mexican entrepreneur about $22, the U.S. or Mexican smuggler about $33, the major U.S. dealer about $200, and the petty U.S. dealer about $500. These prices fluctuate somewhat. A kilo in a border town costs about $75, and many users simply skip the U.S. middlemen and go down to a border town to buy a kilo or two for a group of friends. The bulk of arrests for smuggling are of these small operators.

Illegal drug *users* in the San Diego, California, area in 1970 were predominantly young (average age about 18 years), male, Anglos. Women were arrested primarily due to their associations with their husbands or boyfriends rather than as independent users. There is very little illegal drug use among the Spanish surname population, and it is almost nonexistent among older or female Spanish surname people.

Arrests for *smuggling* from Mexico into the U.S. in the Tijuana-San Diego vicinity are about evenly divided between Anglo and Spanish surname people, but the Spanish surname people tend to be much more professional at smuggling and to be carrying larger loads. Drug smugglers in the area tend to be older than users. The average age of Anglo smugglers is about 24 years, and that of Spanish surname smugglers, about 30 years. Anglo women are rarely involved in smuggling, while it is somewhat common for older Spanish surname women to be caught smuggling.

Nationally, the over 4,000 drug smugglers arrested annually in the U.S. are divided into 14 percent with "dangerous drugs" such as amphetamines, barbiturates, and LSD; 16 percent with the "true narcotics" such as heroin and cocaine; and 70 percent with marijuana. The San Ysidro area has a recent average daily arrest record of about five persons and average daily confiscations of several thousand units of dangerous drugs, just less than one ounce of heroin, and about 110 pounds of marijuana. These averages distort the picture somewhat because some very large drug seizures are included, while most smugglers try to carry across only a few kilos of marijuana or a few plastic bags filled with pills.

A few Anglos have recently been involved in large-scale commercial smuggling. Some Anglos use planes to fly over and drop their loads for pickup by trucks or small, private fishing boats that simply load or unload at the docks. Several seizures ("busts"), for example, were made of commercial quantities of drugs in the Tijuana-San Diego area in May 1970: 1,095 pounds of marijuana on a boat off the California coast near San Luis Obispo; 9,000 pounds of marijuana on two barges near Long Beach; more than 3 million pills of dangerous drugs in the specially built compartments of a truck near the border; and $2.4 million worth of heroin in a house in Tijuana. The later seizure involved a predominantly Spanish surname gang of 10, with 39 other accomplices.

According to the Mexicans the Anglos make all the mistakes. They deal in the border towns where police surveillance is greater, problems with informers are greater, and frauds (such as taking the money and not delivering or selling packaged alfalfa) are more frequent. They dress and act like hippies; they hang around and talk openly about marijuana. They use their own cars or panel trucks and station wagons that the customs inspectors figured out years ago. They buy from strangers. And they try to cross while reeking with the smell of marijuana on their clothes and in the car. Marijuana has such a distinctive odor that U.S. Customs has been able to train dogs to detect its presence with great precision.

The Mexican dealers avoid the hippie community and prefer to operate simply as middlemen and transporters. They hire unknown and otherwise innocent workers and housewives as "mules" to drive the load across the border. The mules are given very little information, usually just a telephone number which they are instructed to call when they arrive at their destination in the U.S. When they call, they are then told where to leave the load and where they can pick up their pay.

The Sale of Drugs in Tijuana

San Ysidro is unimportant in general commercial import-export trade, handling only about one-tenth of 1 percent of recorded U.S. imports and exports. Also the traffic in drugs is only a minor part of the total commercial activities of Tijuana. Manufacturing industries have become important, but tourism is still the major industry of the city. It is under the cover of the great flow of tourists that the drug smuggling takes place. San Ysidro, California, across from Tijuana, Baja California, is the busiest port-of-entry for persons in the United States. Although the U.S.-Mexico border is over 2,500 miles long and has 31 "ports-of-entry," the Tijuana-San Ysidro crossing carries the largest flow of illicit drugs from Mexico to the U.S. This has promoted Tijuana as a commercial center for this drug traffic. Dealers come from all parts of North America to buy and sell drugs in Tijuana. The five Mexican federal investigators in Tijuana deal with the heaviest drug traffic in Mexico. In three and one-half years they seized over 50 tons of marijuana and 50 kilograms of heroin.

Dealers in Tijuana sell marijuana primarily by the kilo brick, rather than by the "lid" (ounce baggie) or "joint" (cigarette). Taxi drivers, bartenders, and other contacts often sell retail amounts of amphetamines or the other common "dangerous drugs," but they generally do not sell retail quantities of marijuana or the opiates. In fact, taxi drivers and the other people in commerce along the tourist street Avenida Revolucion are rarely dealers themselves, although they may be agents for the dealers. The taxi driver takes the customer to the dealer. The drug traffic in Tijuana is never seen by the usual tourist or even the average Tijuanese, just as the ordinary citizens of Toronto or San Francisco never see the drug commerce in their own city. The use of drugs by Mexicans today is uncommon. The Mexican "hippies" who hang around the dance clubs along Avenida Revolucion seem to be more interested in the liberated young American women than drugs. For the city as a whole the material involved in this commerce is irrelevant, except that the city's reputation suffers.

There are basic reasons why Tijuana developed into the major entrepôt for the marijuana traffic from Mexico to the United States. A large market for marijuana has developed in recent years in California, Tijuana receives more American tourists than any other Mexican city, and Tijuana is now a large and impersonal city. Marijuana, heroin, and cocaine are available under surreptitious conditions, usually by contacts who operate outside of the tourist center. All of these drugs are available in commercial quantities at prices that promote smuggling into the United States.

Mexican public sentiment and police vigilance have increasingly moved against the drug traffic. Thus, several pharmacies have been closed down in Tijuana because of their sale of amphetamines and barbiturates in bulk quantities to U.S. citizens without a prescription. Unlawful possession of pills, usually in bulk quantities, is one of the most common reasons for the arrest of Americans in Tijuana. Originally Mexican law was extended for the sake of the U.S. Mexico generally has not required prescriptions, but in this case Tijuana authorities responded to help solve America's problem of illicit drug imports. Then the State of Baja California moved one step further and now requires doctor's prescriptions for the sale of all dangerous drugs in the state, to Mexicans as well as aliens. The latter regulation is no longer seen as simply a protection of American tourists because it is feared that the California drug-using subculture is fostering the development of a counterpart in Tijuana, along with a diffusion of long hair for young men, "rock" music, and "mod" dress.

One small firm in Chicago sold billions of amphetamines and other dangerous drugs over a period of ten years to two Tijuana "pharmaceutical distributors," one of which was a completely fictitious company with an address approximately on the 11th hole of the Tijuana County Club. The owner of that fictitious company was known as the "pep-pill king of Tijuana." His brother owned a second pharmaceutical distributorship, a pharmacy. In 1970 U.S. agents impounded 1.3 million amphetamines in 13 barrels in San Ysidro from this Chicago firm.

In February and March 1969 some 2,000 Mexican police and federal troops developed the annual campaign to discover and destroy the main sources of narcotics in Mexico. An estimated 47 million opium-producing plants in 2,701 poppy fields were located and destroyed in the campaign. Over 33 tons of marijuana were burned, and 1,615 drug arrests were made by federal police during the year, including 130 U.S. citizens. A similar sweep in 1970 used 15,000 soldiers and over the year destroyed some 6,000 acres of poppies and 44 tons of marijuana. This is not some kind of peaceful agricultural program for the Mexicans. Scores of Mexican army men have lost their lives in gun battles with narcotics farmers and middlemen.

Legislation and Jurisdictions

U.S. federal laws say that the unauthorized importing of marijuana, opium, heroin, morphine, and cocaine is a felony, and the first conviction carries a 5-20-year prison sentence and up to $20,000 in fines, without probation or parole (Title 21 of the U.S. Code). Dangerous drugs (LSD, amphetamines, and such) are covered under smuggling of merchandise (Title 18 of the U.S. Code), and a violation carries a sentence of 1-5 years imprisonment and fines determined by the value of the smuggled goods, with the possibility of probation and parole.

Generally a smuggler is convicted only once for a single crime and under only one set of laws, but the laws differ and the situation involves inherent jurisdictional conflict. The various legal agencies have had to develop a working agreement. The military services have tended to prosecute their own people when the crime was possession or smuggling for use rather than for sale. For example, the U.S. Navy has had an arrangement with the Customs authorities at San Ysidro to prosecute itself the five to six Navy men a month who have been found smuggling narcotics from Tijuana rather than the civil courts doing so. The difference between "for use" and "for sale" is arbitrarily determined by the quantity possessed, so that "for use" is variously said to be 5 ounces to 1 kilo or less of marijuana or 1,000 to 2,000 units or less of dangerous drugs. The state tends to prosecute U.S. civilians who are caught smuggling drugs into California for their own use, usually as just a misdemeanor. Smugglers of larger quantities tend to be turned over to the federal government for prosecution. Mexican citizens caught at the border may be tried by either U.S. or Mexican courts, but they usually prefer U.S. courts because the release on bail, probation, and parole policies are more lenient and U.S. prisons tend to be more comfortable than Mexican prisons.

Laws protecting the average citizen from being stopped and searched without reason do not apply at the border. And the application of search and seizure without due cause is expanding. Now if a person is considered to be under constant surveillance after leaving the border zone, he is considered to be under border jurisdiction as far as the search and seizure laws apply. Because the border station is legally a zone for search and seizure and most arrested violators are caught in the act of smuggling, the conviction rate of those arrested is over 90 percent.

Since the federal laws on marijuana and hard narcotics are much more severe than local laws and the assignment of those arrested to the various agencies is arbitrary, the smuggler is at the potentially capricious mercy of the border station personnel. This fact is a police advantage in the sense that it can be used as a leverage to elicit cooperation from the smuggler to tell about his source of the drug. It could, however, be a disadvantage in terms of the equality of the law to smugglers who have surly, uncooperative personalities. Also, the investigative personnel have leverage on the suspect even within a single court system because they can recommend leniency to the judge.

Federal law allows border patrolmen in search for aliens illegally in the U.S. to enter any property, except private homes, within 25 miles of the border and to search without a warrant. Federal law also gives immigration officers authority to board and search vessels in territorial waters and other vehicles within a "reasonable distance" of international borders. This is usually considered to be 100 miles unless the surveillance is "continuous," in which case there is no limit.

Detection within the border station depends to a large degree on the inspector's ability to spot the patterns of nervousness that are commonly associated with amateur smuggling. There are little psychological clues in eye behavior, the speed of speech, unnatural silence, overfriendliness, being flushed under emotional pressure, and so on that are common clues. They say, "Where he hides the stuff is less important than how he behaves." The professional smugglers understand this and concentrate on producing an impression of innocence, a "plausible performance." And the inspectors know this too, their incapacity to detect just from behavior, so they randomly add careful searches of unsuspicious people. The older inspectors tend to be more successful than the younger staff in detecting smugglers, but they are inarticulate about why they are more successful. The older inspectors place a lot of weight on their "experience" and "intuition" without really understanding why they are more successful.

Inspectors are not supposed to search the clothing or body of persons entering the U.S. unless they have a "real suspicion" that the person is carrying contraband. However, this suspicion may not always be based on objective, articulable facts. In one San Diego case in 1970 the prosecution argued that

> Federal officers performing inspection duties at the port of entry frequently must rely on intuitive reactions based on their peculiar knowledge and experience regarding border traffic, in considering whether there should be more careful examinations.

To demonstrate their case the prosecution said that in fiscal 1969 only .016 percent (4,811) of the people crossing the Mexican border were personally searched. Of the people searched, 23 percent (892 men and 375 women) were actually carrying contraband on their persons, and in 69 percent of the cases some form of smuggling was attempted. The argument was that very few personal searches are made and that those that are made are not done capriciously, even when the inspector cannot articulate precisely why the search has been called for.

Smuggling and Detection Techniques

Low-flying planes, boats, underwater swimmers, and back-packing hikers have all been used recently, but they stand out and have a high detection rate. The majority of smuggling takes place directly in the presence of the Customs officials, primarily by concealment in vehicles. Commercial amounts of marijuana are quite bulky and are thus usually carried over in specially built compartments in the gas tank, seats, floors, trunks, or engine areas. These are detected by visual inspection, pounding suspicious parts for sounds, and finally dismantling suspicious sections. Smaller quantities are often placed inside other articles or in small parts like air cleaners.

A detection technique of considerable potential is the use of trained dogs to sniff out narcotics. The FBI used dogs to detect opium over twenty years ago, but they dropped the program when it was found that the dogs were becoming addicted. With marijuana there is no addiction threat, so German shepherds are successfully being used to sniff it out. An "association collar" is used that makes the dog relate to the task of sniffing for marijuana. The dogs can detect both raw marijuana and the smell of marijuana smoke, so that even clothes or cars that have acquired the smell can be detected.

Heroin and cocaine comes in such small quantities that it is much more easily hidden than marijuana. Heroin is often hidden on the smuggler's body, but the border station maintains rooms where certain suspects are required to strip for a body inspection by one of the station's medical staff. Larger smuggling operations employ carriers or "mules" to take the goods across the border. Drugs are also sometimes placed in a tourist's car and picked up by following the tourist until he stops on the American side.

Detection techniques include the use of double inspections, both paid and unpaid informants, undercover agents, and the "blitz," a brief, intensive search of all vehicles and persons crossing the border. There are also Border Patrol check stations farther into California on Interstate 5 and U.S. 395. These are primarily to look for illegal aliens, but they also discover contraband drugs at these stations. An important detection aid is that the U.S. employs salaried Mexican agents who work in Mexico to tip off the U.S. investigative agencies when a shipment is coming across.

Detection agencies tend to be overly bureaucratic and secretive. Their techniques are handed down primarily by word-of-mouth, with very little emphasis on the scientific development of detection procedures. They are task oriented rather than research oriented, so they are not very objective about their own work. Still, by their own admission they are unable to detect 85-95 percent of the drug traffic that passes through the border station. There is also a need for greater cooperation between the U.S. and Mexican detection and judicial agencies. For example, when in March 1969 Mexican agents arrested a known Mexican smuggler with $250,000 worth of heroin, the Mexican judge released the smuggler on the basis of testimony that made it appear that U.S. agents had entered Mexico and planted the narcotics where the smuggler just happened to be rabbit hunting near Tecate. The head of the California Narcotics Bureau said that Mexican agents were cooperating in the investigation, they knew where and when the smuggler was to come across, and that the American agents never entered Mexico.

Most of the training comes through the experience of being at a station and hearing the specifics of one "bust" after another. Smuggling patterns are learned out of this. The inspectors can also rely on informers, who receive a "moiety," a reward paid by the Treasury Department. Although "moiety" literally means "half," actually it is up to 25 percent of the sum recovered, though not more than $50,000, and usually about 5-10 percent of the value on expensive items. The first person who informs Customs about a smuggler receives the full moiety rather than a division among several informers. To cut through the bureaucratic red tape for speedy payoffs and to protect the secrecy of Mexican informers, the San Ysidro station has a "contingency fund" from which the officials can immediately pay an informer in cash.

Operation Intercept

Operation Intercept was a coordinated effort by several U.S. law enforcement agencies to reduce the illicit flow of drugs into the U.S. from Mexico. It induced a brief trauma in U.S.-Mexico relations, between September 21 and October 11 in 1969, that is useful as a case study in the ethnology of international relations. The use of illegal drugs was becoming a major political issue when President Nixon established a Task Force on Narcotics. In mid-August 1969 the Task Force made these formal recommendations on controlling the traffic from Mexico:

1. The data on individual smugglers should be analyzed to determine the typical traits of smugglers so that predictions can be improved.

2. Case histories of smuggling operations should be analyzed to determine identifiable characteristic patterns of smugglers.

3. U.S. citizens traveling just to the Mexican border cities should be encouraged to leave their cars in the U.S. and to enter and leave Mexico on foot. This could be encouraged by providing additional parking facilities at border-crossing points.

4. Existing fences along the border should be extended.

5. Many border stations need more physical area within which to operate.

6. The Department of Defense should consider placing Tijuana off-limits to military personnel.

7. Any aliens who are narcotic drug addicts or who have been convicted on drug-related charges should be prevented from entering the U.S.

8. A study should be conducted of the effectiveness of existing detection methods, and an economical and practical perimeter detection device should be developed.

9. The use of aircraft for smuggling is increasing, but this is being fought by the air intelligence center at Yuma, Arizona, where data on 73,000 private aircraft and pilots are catalogued. The Immigration and Naturalization Service currently employs twenty planes along the Mexican border.

Operation Intercept coordinated and strengthened policing efforts of all international traffic along the border. Land, sea, and air traffic were all carefully surveyed. At the San Ysidro station 83 men were added for the operation. The Coast Guard was alerted, and inspections at the 27 airports at which U.S.-Mexico international flights are authorized to land were strengthened. Each vehicle entering the U.S. was supposed to be given a two-minute primary inspection, instead of a 15-20 second primary inspection. This increase in inspection time slowed down the traffic until there were massive traffic jams.

The time to cross the border at San Ysidro during much of the daytime and evening hours increased to as much as two hours. Mexicans who work in the U.S. were hours late for their jobs, and many Mexican students were forced to miss their classes in San Diego. Mexicans virtually stopped shopping in the U.S. because of the long wait unless they had to go across for other reasons. An international conference on border problems was cancelled, in part as a protest by the Mexican side.

American tourism rapidly declined. The Tijuana merchants of tourist goods reported business declines of around 80 percent. Avenida Revolucion was almost deserted. As the days wore on, feelings of resentment toward the U.S. built up along the Mexican border. Then a number of spontaneous programs of retaliation against the U.S. began to spring up. Individual merchants said things like "Our merchants and people are getting together to stop shopping in the U.S. We want the Americans to know what it is like." Some officials in the Mexican immigration office claimed that they would retaliate by enforcing a health check, requiring vaccination certificates, and "turn away the American drug addicts from Mexico."

By October 1 the local politicians were involved. The Governor of California spoke out in favor of Operation Intercept. The Juarez Chamber of Commerce and the mayor of Juarez organized a retaliation movement called Operation Dignity to go into effect along the border at 9:00 p.m., October 2. This was a boycott of retail business in the U.S., and appeals went to chambers of commerce in all border cities to ask the local people to do all their shopping on the Mexican side of the border. This program was never very successful, and the Mexican chambers of commerce along the border shifted to a letter-writing campaign. They distributed 100,000 copies of a letter addressed to the U.S. President calling for an end to Operation Intercept and for more inspection personnel to speed up the border traffic. The letters were given primarily to U.S. citizens to mail in.

The Tijuana students entered the protest somewhat later than the businessmen and politicians, but they protested in person by picketing the U.S. border station. On the evening of October 7 about 150 Tijuana high-school and college students demonstrated at the border against Operation Intercept. They talked to Mexicans as they drove up to the station and tried to talk them into turning back. They explained that they were doing their part in Operation Dignity. They got very little publicity, however, because the U.S. newsmen who went to cover the story were stopped by the Mexican police and pictures were not allowed. The police said that the newsmen needed a permit to take pictures in the border-station area, the permits were issued only by the Mexican immigration office, and the immigration office was closed until morning.

The chambers of commerce in Baja California did not agree with the strategy of Operation Dignity. They said that these international differences and problems should be settled at the government level, not by boycotts, which would just make matters worse. Tijuana's businessmen asked the Mexican federal officials to intensify searches for drugs carried by the traffic moving northward from central Mexico, especially along Mexico's Highway 15. The local branch of the dominant political party, Partido Revolucionario Institucional, demanded that Mexico's federal officials move swiftly to burn the fields of poppies and marijuana.

The U.S. government became increasingly concerned by the reaction to Operation Intercept on both sides of the border. By October 8 U.S. Attorney Ed Miller was sent on a speaking tour "to help cool the rhetoric." Other U.S. officials before him had said that the operation was to cut the flow of illegal drugs enough to raise the prices of drugs and to decrease their consumption in the U.S. This seemed like a very incomplete explanation to many people along the border.

Attorney Miller said that

> The primary purpose of Operation Intercept is to acquaint the Mexican government with the gravity of the narcotics problem at the international border and to show them that the U.S. government is willing to use all its resources to beat it.

Operation Intercept apparently was a strategy to pressure the Mexicans into cooperating with the U.S. in the solution of the U.S. drug problem. His plea was directed to the

Mexican government to locate and destroy the marijuana and poppy fields, stem the flow along Highways 2 and 15, and prosecute the major Mexican suppliers.

Miller said that after years of prodding by his department the Department of Justice sent officers to San Diego for a personnel investigation early in 1969.

> They were taken on a tour of Tijuana and when they saw that they could buy marijuana at any time, any place, and from almost any cab driver, the message of the seriousness of the local narcotics got through to them. The officials saw that our list of the license plates of known smugglers had reached unmanageable proportions; our informants just could not keep up with the known smugglers or supply us information fast enough.

On October 11, after a meeting with Mexican officials in Washington, the U.S. called off the operation "in order to eliminate unnecessary inconvenience, delay, and irritation." The U.S. renamed the new phase "Operation Cooperation." The additional line inspectors were taken off. The Coast Guard and other military units that were helping, including such things as radar scans along parts of the border, were taken off their assignments.

At the end of the year the 21 days of Operation Intercept had very little impact on annual statistical data: Tijuana's economic position was as healthy as ever, the number of border crossings had continued its usual annual increase, and the volume of drugs from Mexico continued to increase over the previous year. Monthly profiles, of course, showed an unusual dip in September and October. A change, however, did come in attitudes. The news coverage, talk, and emotional stress of those days strongly enforced the idea that the drug traffic is really a serious business that we have to do something about. The U.S. was successful in forcing the Mexicans to take the drug traffic more seriously, so that it became a major issue in Mexican politics in 1970. Each political party vowed to eliminate the drug traffic.

In November 1969 a computerized vehicle-license-check

system was put into operation at the San Ysidro station. The U.S. government is now installing this system at every vehicle port-of-entry on the U.S.-Mexico border. The computer can handle 125 simultaneous messages, so it will have sufficient capacity to handle vehicle traffic for years to come since there are only 86 primary inspection lanes for vehicles on the Mexican border. The license number of each vehicle that enters the primary inspection station is relayed to a central computer which contains data, by vehicle license number, or previous and suspected smugglers. If a license number is entered which, according to the computer's memory banks, is being used by a suspected smuggler, then the computer system sends back a visual reply to the line inspector of "Hit! Hit! Hit!" The computer then prints out the details of the previous convictions of the suspected smuggler. Inside the office of the supervisor of inspectors a bell goes off and a light indicates which particular lane of traffic received a "Hit" reply. The suspected vehicle and its occupants are then carefully moved into a secondary inspection zone.

It now looks very much like a war is going on within the U.S. and Mexico, a revolution from the point of view of those sympathetic with the drug-using subculture and a battle against the spectre of moral decay and organized crime from the government point of view. However perceived, the use of warlike phrases such as Operation Intercept, Operation Cooperation, and Operation Checkpoint is fully appropriate. This drive should have a long-range impact on the screening of goods that enter the U.S., to increase generally both the monitoring and the restrictions on the inward flow of goods.

vi: *Life in Tijuana 's Prison*

The Mexican penal system officially allows much greater interaction between inmates and their outside friends and relatives than is generally allowed in the United States or Canada. For example, long and private visits by the prisoner's spouse or whole family are regularly permitted throughout Mexico. Children born to female inmates while they are in prison may be raised for years in the prison. Large quantities of food, clothing, and other goods are carried in to the prisoners by relatives.

Rather than generate a highly disciplined program for the prisoners, the officials allow a fairly self-disciplining prison subculture to form, largely along lines that parallel the culture of the lower social class of the wider society. The extensive interaction with the outside and the permissiveness within the prison promotes the development of an elaborate free-enterprise economy within the prison. Within this economic system a prisoner's wealth, industriousness, and bartering ability determine the nature of his food, living quarters, dress, and social status.

The prison in Tijuana is particularly useful as a study in border institutions because it has a large number of American prisoners. Americans usually undergo great cultural shock when they are incarcerated in Mexican prisons. In addition to the stress of confinement, they generally cannot speak Spanish, they do not understand Mexican customs, and they abhor what are essentially lower-class Mexican food, housing, and standards of medicine and cleanliness. However, Americans form alliances with other Americans and, due to their greater wealth, are usually among the prison's elite. La Mesa Penitenciaria in eastern Tijuana is the major prison of the Mexican state of Baja California (Boysen, 1970; Demaris, 1970).

Only about one-tenth of 1 percent of the Americans who come to the Tijuana-Ensenada area are arrested by the various police agencies. The vast majority of these are for traffic violations or misdemeanors such as drunk and disorderly, disrespect for police officials, and urinating in a public place. The standard penalty for these misdemeanors is a $24 fine. When the annual tourist traffic is 11 million, even one-tenth of 1 percent comes to the large figure of 11,000 people, and an average of about 5,500 Americans are actually held each year. Finally, there are roughly 25 Americans who are accused of felonies and are sent to La Mesa Penitenciaria each year to wait a few months until their trials come up and serve out their sentences if they are convicted. Most felonies are not bailable in Mexico.

The most frequently committed felony by Americans in Baja California is possession or the attempt to purchase marijuana or other illegal drugs, which carries a minimum sentence of three years of imprisonment. Then, in order of frequency with their minimum sentences in months, Americans are committed to La Mesa Penitenciaria for attempting to pass counterfeit U.S. currency or fraud (over 3,000 pesos, 36 months), grand theft (over 500 pesos, 24 months), and other crimes (assault, 12; abortion, 3-12; rape, 6; and murder, 24-240). The most common felony of the Mexicans in Baja California is grand theft, especially armed robbery, but about one-quarter of these are by heroin addicts and are in fact drug-related crimes.

In 1968 the prison had the following estimated composition of inmates by nationality, sex, and age. In addition to 725 Mexicans and 40 Americans, there were 35 Cubans, Filipinos, and other Spanish speaking prisoners. Twenty-five of the Mexicans and one American were women. The average age of the prisoners was in the 30s, with an age range from 18 to 70 years.

Description of the Prison

La Mesa Penitenciaria was built in 1961. The outside is a double concrete block wall with a walkway along the top. It is the size of a city block, 350 feet on each side. The walls are about 15 feet high with wooden watchtowers at the corners and the center of each wall. The prison buildings are close to this wall on the inside, leaving a large, open court in the center. The only entrance is through a heavy-gauge chain-link gate, which leads to a small reception yard where visitors register. To the right of the reception yard are rooms where visitors are inspected for weapons, narcotics, and alcoholic beverages. After inspection they continue on through a second chain-link gate to the central courtyard.

Around the wall, in a clockwise direction from the entrance, the main prison buildings are offices, four large commercial workshops, an apartment complex, other shops, another apartment building, the main Corral with its four sleeping quarters or "tanks," a kitchen, a bakery, the solitary confinement cells, a restaurant, a tortilla shop, more apartments, a barber shop, a market, the infirmary, and the self-contained women's quarters. As a part of the scene is a mix of clapboard, stucco, and concrete construction; other tiny cubicles with stores, a barber shop, and a shoeshine stand; and the scattered groups of prisoners. Looking across the large, central dirt plaza one rarely sees more than 200 men because most stay in workshops or their quarters.

The warden is politically appointed for a six-year term. It is considered to be an important appointment because, in addition to his salary, he also draws off money from the internal prison economy. Because of the very low budget given to run the prison, the warden's role seems to be to keep the prisoners contained, alive, and at peace with each other.

Under the warden are four commandants, one of whom is always on duty at the prison. Then, under the commandants are 50 guards, 2 matrons, and several clerical workers. The rest of the work in the prison is done by the prisoners. The guards dress in a uniform style that is common among Mexican police, beige trousers and tan shirts. The guards are officially paid $3.30 per day and work shifts of 24 hours on and 24 hours off. They often carry rifles or pistols in the prison, especially at night, but there is very little friction between guards and prisoners. Two reasons for this amiability seem to be that the guards are culturally close to the prisoners and are selected for their physical prowess, tending to be larger and stronger than the prisoners. Some guards have previously been prisoners at La Mesa Penitenciaria. Several prisoners playfully took the pistol away from a guard in the courtyard and teased him with it for several minutes before returning it. They were not punished.

The guards have well defined social and economic roles within the prison. They carry out the collections of money from the prisoners for the sale of blankets, beds, apartments, the use of shower facilities, and the weekly prison upkeep donations (*talacha*). These are the common *mordidas*, literally "little bites," that prisoners pay. The guards can also procure illegal goods, such as narcotics, and illegal services, such as female inmates as prostitutes, for prisoners with the money to pay for them. In fact, the relationship between the guards and the prisoners is so familiar that the warden must insure against a guard allowing an escape by maintaining that he will see that the responsible guard will serve out the rest of the escapee's sentence.

The infirmary is staffed by prisoners. The head of the infirmary is serving a sentence for having performed abortions. Medical care is free from 6:00-7:00 a.m. and 3:00-4:00 p.m., but it is crowded at these times and all services are charged for at other times. The most prominent chronic medical problems among the prisoners are, in order of importance, drug addiction, veneral disease, tuberculosis, and hepatitis. An inmate delivered a child in the prison infirmary, and she has been allowed to keep and raise the child in the prison for over a year.

When prisoners enter the prison they simply register. There is no physical examination nor are they issued a uniform. They simply wear the clothes they came in. At this time they are required to buy their living accomodations, including blankets, beds, and sleeping quarters. Although prices vary somewhat according to the prisoner's ability to pay, the usual fees in one of the dormitory tanks are a few dollars for a bedroll on the floor, $35 for a cot, and $100 for a choice bunkbed. For more money prisoners may stay in individual apartments called *caracas*, from $200 for a makeshift clapboard room to $500 for a new concrete-block *caraca*. In 1968 one well-to-do Mexican had a second-floor *caraca* with a stairway to his own rooftop patio with a sunshade, several chairs, a barbecue brazier, and potted plants. One count showed 55 of these *caracas*, but there is a continuous building program to accommodate wealthy newcomers. Also, tiny makeshift apartments have recently been constructed in two of the tanks out of plywood and cardboard.

If the prisoner has no money at all he simply sleeps in his clothes on the floor of a tank. There are four two story tanks that are surrounded by a tall chain-link fence. This is the Corral. The few prisoners who are real security risks, regardless of their wealth, are contained in this Corral area or in the solitary confinement cells. Outside of the Corral there is a newer two-story tank arranged so that each floor is a long corridor of double bunkbeds. This structure was built by a Mexican contractor while he was a prisoner. The poorer tanks have no place for the storage of personal belongings, so these are kept in the prisoner's bedroll.

The old tanks are extremely crowded, poorly lighted, and have dirt floors. There is so much cardboard and light wood in internal construction and loose scrap in these areas that fires frequently sweep through a tank. These chaotic conditions enabled two Mexicans and an American to dig a 20-foot tunnel from their tank to outside the wall over a period of several weeks and successfully escape. They would have completed the tunnel much faster except that they had to gradually dispose of the dirt within the prison as they dug. There have been a few other escapes over the wall.

The *caracas* may be furnished any way that the prisoner can afford and the small space permits. The *caracas* are usually seven by nine feet with one window and a door. Most of them are furnished with at least a single or a double bunkbed, a hot plate, and a radio. Some of them add things such as a television receiver, books, a musical instrument, and a refrigerator. Several of the prisoners keep dogs as pets, and many of the *caraca* dwellers pay a prisoner to be his servant. The servants run errands, fix meals, and clean the tiny apartment.

There are several possible arrangements for food. Standard prison fare is prepared by a group of prisoners in the prison kitchen and is served free to the approximately 700 state prisoners in the prison. The typical daily menu of the prison kitchen is roll, coffee, and oatmeal for breakfast; roll and soup for lunch; and roll, coffee, and beans for supper. Anyone with money supplements this with food from other sources. At mealtimes each prisoner brings a bowl that he has fashioned from a tin can or a plastic container into which the food is ladled. There is no dining room; the men simply squat on the ground or lean against a wall to eat.

The 20 or so prisoners who are in the prison for federal crimes are given three and one-half pesos per day (28 cents) to buy the standard prison fare or to buy food from other sources in the prison: six grocery stores, two restaurants, and a tortilla shop. Until the fall of 1969 there were also four prisoners who sold food from small handcarts (*carretónes*) within the prison. This special arrangement for the federal prisoners was established to avoid the local mismanagement of food money.

Friends and relatives bring in sacks of food, which, in addition to providing food for the prisoner they visit, is extensively used in the prison barter system. Objects, particularly food, become the means of obtaining other desired items. The exchange can be a simple matter involving only a few minutes discussion or it can develop over days and involve three or four items. Acquiring a new mattress, or a refrigerator, or a television set may involve weeks of negotiations and *mordida* payments. However, the men have plenty of time and many of them enjoy the competitive gamesmanship of bartering. The convict who acquires goods and services through skillful bartering is admired. Drug addicts are despised when they sell for a pittance bags of groceries that their relatives bring to them. Food is also the most commonly stolen item, not so much to eat the food, but because it can be bartered off for some desired item, such as drugs, a knife, a blanket, or a shirt.

There are several commercial workshops where prisoners may earn $1.50 a day. Several private companies lease space within the prison, supply the necessary materials, and pay the prison a fixed amount for each item that is produced. These workshops produce such things as carved wooden furniture, bed frames, tambourines, bongo drums, and carved miniature wooden ships. A "service fee" is taken out of the worker's paychecks, for the prison officials collect *mordidas* on the workshop industries from both the companies and the workers. No one is required to work and none of the Americans do. However, if a prisoner's visitors do not bring enough food for barter or money itself, the economic demands of the prison force most of the inmates into some kind of gainful employment in the workshops, the food shops, as servants for others, or in the drug trade.

Another regular monetary demand is the *talacha*, a donation toward the upkeep and repair of the prison. This averages about two dollars a week for everyone who does not have a regular job in maintenance, the kitchen, or the infirmary. Those in the *caracas* pay an additional 5 cents to use the toilet and 25 cents to take a shower (15-minute limit for both) or a flat $1.50 per week for the use of the toilet and shower facilities.

One of the most pervasive economic demands within the prison is for drugs of all kinds, although the heroin trade is by far the most significant. The summer 1968 estimates by prisoner informants of the number of heroin addicts in the prison with a need for a daily "fix" were around 200 Mexicans and 16 Americans. By August 1970 the estimates were around 250 Mexicans and 15 Americans. It appears that about one-fourth of the Mexican prisoners are taking heroin.

Most of these men buy a small packet of diluted heroin for $1, called a "paper," each day from a "dealer," usually in the late afternoon. All of the dealers in 1970 were Mexicans. There was one major dealer on the north side of the prison and another one on the south side. Each had a gang of several convict guards and "runners," and each gang tended to stay in its own territory. While each of these dealers sells about 100 "papers" a day, there are also several other smaller dealers.

Prison Routines

There is a morning (about 7:30 a.m.) and an evening (about 7:30 p.m.) roll call (*lista*) in domicile groups and a general cleanup period after each meal. The doors to the tanks are locked at night between the evening and morning roll calls, and *caraca* dwellers are not allowed out at night except to go to the lavatory with the permission of the guards. Other than these formalities the prisoners are on their own to work, lounge, or play at sports. Some prisoners spend hours gossiping, gambling for petty stakes with dominoes or cards, or just strolling back and forth across the prison grounds. The Americans get particularly lethargic and depressed, often "tuning out" the ugliness and noise of the prison by reading or watching television. Some of the prisoners have organized themselves into baseball and soccer leagues that play a schedule of games in the central court.

The prison routine is broken somewhat by visiting days, the visit by a Catholic priest once a week, and occasional small feasts. A Protestant missionary couple comes in once a week, and there is a small church in the Corral, Iglesia de Dios en Christo. At times on busy Sunday visiting days one gets the feeling he is in a bustling Mexican village or on a side street in Tijuana. You see large family groups, and since they do not wear uniforms, the prisoners do not stand out. There are children playing. The jukebox blares from one restaurant. People play guitars or have their radios turned on. Some of the craftsmen try to sell their carvings to the visitors. In one case a group of prisoners purchased a live pig which they cooked in the prison yard. A goat and a cow are left to forage between an internal fence and the outside wall. On another occasion a woman visitor with bags of groceries set up an umbrella and a large cooking pot over a fire in the courtyard and proceeded to make tamales.

Tuesday is "conjugal day," when the wives or girlfriends of prisoners may visit. Only those who own or can borrow the use of a *caraca* have much opportunity for sexual intercourse. On Thursday and Sunday prisoners may receive as many visitors as they want. In each case the visitors stay a long time and freely mingle with the prisoners. Visitors may enter any time from 9:00 a.m. to 12:30 p.m. and leave any time from 12:30 p.m. to 3:00 p.m. The average number of visitors is roughly 50 on Tuesdays, 140 on Thursdays, and 250 on Sundays.

Fights are commonplace in the tanks, primarily over petty thievery, verbal slights, and to establish status through physical prowess. Fights between *caraca* dwellers are uncommon, but one occurred when a prisoner's large mongrel dog attacked another's tiny terrier. There was a knife fight over the use of the pay telephone. One San Diego gang member was awaiting trial for the shooting of another young San Diegan in Mexico. While in the prison he was stabbed to death on the basketball court by another prisoner he had known on the outside.

A woman who regularly visits her husband in the prison was getting tired of going there because "It seems that all they talk about is who they fought with and who slashed who." The most common causes for being sent to solitary confinement (*las tombas*, "the tombs") are chronic fighting or stealing. This is a concrete block building with six small cells (about five by ten feet), each with a heavy door with a tiny slot for light and ventilation.

A recurrent theme of the prisoners' conversations relate to social groups and social status among the prisoners. In word play Mexicans call Americans *gabacho* ("Frenchy"), while the Americans reciprocate with "greaser." A person's status on the outside has very little direct influence on his status in the prison. Wealth is the major determinant of social status within the prison, so that a destitute medical doctor could have a low social position.

Heroin addiction is seen as a negative characteristic that divides the prisoners with a schism that runs through the whole prison society, placing about 250 people in one essentially outcaste group, while the remaining 600 people dominate the affairs of the prison society. This cleavage is more important than language, nationality, or personality in determining whom a person associates with, because "clean" (nonaddicted) people simply do not get friendly with "hypes" (from hypodermic).

Heroin addicts are not despised so much for their compulsive habit *per se* as for their tendency to be poor and to be completely untrustworthy. The social scale goes up from the poorest tank dwellers to those in the best *caracas*, but personality also influences social status. At the top of the social scale are those with the best *caracas*, the big drug dealers, and the more wealthy. The wealthy are continually badgered for handouts by some prisoners and for "donations" by the prison administration, but they have considerable power to do what they want in the prison.

An enterprising man can make arrangements to receive a woman prisoner into his *caraca* or a workshop in the evening. The arrangement is made on the agreement with a specific woman. Since the women are rather isolated, the most important events in their lives are the visiting days when they can go out into the general courtyard and also these "dates" with the male prisoners. The dates are anticipated with a great amount of preparation and attention to clothing, hairdo, and makeup. They are paid about five dollars per date, of which the guards and matrons receive a small amount. There often develops a fairly continuing relationship between a woman and her regular dates. Women make most of their money in the prison economy by washing and ironing clothes for the male inmates.

Conclusions

This prison contrasts greatly with Canadian and American prisons, primarily because it is allowed to operate as a free-enterprise *market* economy. The inmates are intimately involved in day-to-day economic decisions. They are active participants in a society that is somewhat close to the social realities of a lower-class life outside of the prison.

The economy of Canadian and American prisons is highly *administered*, with a standard issue of uniforms, living facilities, and food. The manifestations of a market economy are largely suppressed in Anglo-American prisons because they are seen as undermining the authority and discipline of the administration. There is an enforced and regimented equality among the prisoners in Anglo-American prisons. Administrators design and carry out a program to inculcate passive obedience, which may be useful in the peaceful operation of a prison but is not a particularly useful preparation for life outside the prison.

At La Mesa Penitenciaria inmates receive income in the

form of goods and money from visiting friends and relatives; by working in a workshop, a food shop, or as a servant for other prisoners; by successful bartering; or by selling drugs. They must contribute to the maintenance of the prison, but a survival level of food and medical care is free. Beyond that they must pay for their clothing, living quarters, and additional food. Social status in the prison is more correlated with wealth than nationality or other factors. In sum, a strong incentive to earn money comes from the internal prison economy rather than the fear of punishment by the administration. The payment of *mordidas* sanctions and perpetuates in the prison society a practice of circumventing the law. Instead of promoting a legal conscience and a genuine respect for the law among the prisoners the system promotes a set of brutal situational ethics. The extreme inequalities that the system promotes are also inhumane. New inmates who are poor or too sick to work may barely survive. Instead of treating drug addiction the administration has allowed the prison to become an easy place to buy drugs.

It seems that both Anglo-American and Mexican penal systems could learn from each other to arrive at some middle ground between the administered regimentation of American prisons and the inequalities of Mexican prisons. The open-visiting policy of Mexican prisons is a positive feature, and this could still be followed under an equitable administration. Anglo-American penologists could also allow a limited market economy to operate within a prison without undermining its orderly administration. Mexican penologists, finally, need to insist that some regimentation is humane and that disregard for the law within the prison promotes a general disregard for the law in the wider society.

vii: *Tecate:*
Urbanization in the
Shadow of Tijuana

The City and Its Prosperity

Tecate, Mexico, is a small industrial city of 18,000 population located 33 miles east of Tijuana in a valley with a setting of rolling hills and mountains. In an election campaign President Diaz Ordaz called Tecate "La ventana mas limpia de Mexico"—"The cleanest window to Mexico"—and this has become the city's motto. It is 1,600 feet above sea level with a dry mediterranean climate. The Cuauhtemoc Brewry (the producer of Tecate, Carta Blanca, and Bohemia brands of beer), a coffee-processing plant, three electronics assembly plants, Rancho La Puerta (a 1,750-acre diet resort used almost exclusively by Americans three miles west of the town), and the supplying of commercial services to outlying farms and ranches are the major sources of income for the town. Metalurgica California (a manufacturer of steel-construction reinforcement rods), a custom-furniture manufacturing firm, and a ceramic-tile manufacturer are additional sources of employment and income. Tecate has very little tourist trade and thus contrasts greatly with Tijuana (Price, 1967), for developing in the shadow of Tijuana led the people of Tecate actively to avoid tourism.

Tecate was just a ranching center with a small settlement in the early 1900s, but it was located in a fairly well watered valley at the intersection of a good route to Ensenada and the Mexicali-Tijuana road. Also the Southern Pacific Railroad was routed from San Diego to the Tijuana River Valley through Tecate and then back into the U.S. at Campo, to give Tecate an important transport connection with the U.S. The port of entry was established in 1921, a whiskey factory had a brief life in the town during Prohibition in the U.S., and a malt factory was established in 1928. The brewery began in 1944 and stimulated considerable growth in the town. Cerveceria Cuauhtemoc is Tecate's major benefactor. It donated a swimming pool and recreation center for the city's youth. It maintains a large oak-covered park with a playground and a picnic area. Most important, depending on the season it employs 180 to 350 people in its three-shift, seven-day-a-week operation. Pay at the brewery begins at 75 pesos (about $6) a day. The plant now produces 12.5 million cans of Tecate beer a month. Completion of a paved highway to Ensenada in 1954 and the establishment in 1961 of the coffee processor, the packing plant, and a metal-works factory essentially completed the foundation for contemporary Tecate.

The international border runs along the northern part of the valley, and the downtown area of Tecate is built adjacent to the border. The road from the border-crossing point (which connects two miles north to Highway 94 in San Diego County) passes through the town and on to the highway south to Ensenada. An even more important highway passes through the town, paralleling the border, from Tijuana to Mexicali. The existence of this crossroad was crucial for the early development of the town, but now the town would continue to thrive even if the border station was closed to traffic. Except for the cattle and train crossing at Campo this is the only crossing point along the 135 miles between Tijuana and Mexicali. However, in contrast to the large stations at Tijuana and Mexicali serving complex industrial and commercial hinterlands, the border station at Tecate is a small operation with light traffic, mostly local trade, and a relaxed atmosphere.

Tecate, California, on the U.S. side of the line is a small scattering of homes, the border station, a post office, a customs broker, the American Store which sells groceries and clothing, and the Protestant mission. The majority of customers in the American Store come from Tecate, Mexico, and the clerks live there also. The normal language in the store is Spanish. Some 60 percent of the mailboxes in the U.S. Post Office are rented by residents of Tecate, Mexico, to receive mail from their relatives in the U.S. or, for some, to maintain a legal residency in the U.S.

The Tecate Protestant mission is in a curious position because the director was not born in Mexico and is therefore prohibited by the Mexican Constitution from preaching religion in Mexico. The mission has a Mexican assistant who can preach in Mexico and who runs a small bookstore on the Mexican side and a seminary. The Mexican border officials occasionally give the director a little trouble, but he manages to maintain a role as a social worker who gives moral support to the Protestant churches on the Mexican side and, in fact, serves as an important unofficial liaison between several local segments of the Mexican and American societies. The director and his assistant are members of a "third culture" that is neither Mexican nor American but something new that functions to mediate these two cultures.

A few vacant houses on the U.S. side are being rented by Mexicans. Thus, one was rented for temporary storage of goods purchased in the U.S. by the owner of a restaurant in Tecate, Mexico. Another one was rented by a Mexican family to establish a residency in the U.S. so that their high-school-age children could attend school in the U.S.

This accommodation to border conditions operates on both sides of the border. Foreigners may not own real estate within 100 kilometers of the international border, but they can work out lease arrangements. It is difficult to arrange for working visas for foreigners in either country, so a border problem arises when people skirt the law. We found several cases of Mexican men who leave their families in Tecate while they work without visas in the U.S. We also found Americans working in Mexico without visas. For example, instead of outright employment of Americans Rancho La Puerta developed a system of American "co-op" workers who receive room, board, and occasional gifts for their work. This resort also employs about 100 Mexican workers from Tecate.

The hourly wage for unskilled men in Tecate, Mexico, runs high at about 60-85 cents, although maids still work for only about $15 a week. The cost of living is high as well, so for a balanced view we should include comparisons of cost of real goods and services. Tecate is a new and small city, and is relatively weak in influence on the Mexican federal government, typically a major source for funds for public construction. Thus, although it has wealth, Tecate has very poorly developed water, sewer, and road systems. A recent notable exception is the construction with the aid of federal funds of a very beautiful high school in Tecate. The large percentage of families covered by Mexican social security in Tecate (50 percent vs. 10 percent nationally) illustrates the industrial character of the town. Houses in Tecate tend to be larger, more often owned by the occupant, and more often have a television set than in Mexico City.

The significant differences in the kinds of businesses in Tijuana and Tecate are found in Tecate's lack of tourist attractions, wholesalers, and personal services such as doctors, dentists, and laywers. Yet Tecate has 24 restaurants, mostly small so that it actually has a high proportion of "food services and entertainment." And over 75 of Tecate's retailers are registered to purchase products in California for sale in Mexico on an "extax basis," that is, without paying California state sales tax.

The Interview Survey

One of the initial steps in our 1967 study of Tecate was a geographical survey of the town. One of the products of this survey was a map that indicated each housing unit in the town, 1,406 total units. The map was then used as a basis for allocating interview schedule assignments for approximately every fifteenth house in town. An interview schedule that could be administered in one-half an hour was developed from questions submitted by the ten students, translated into Spanish, and then reproduced in enough copies for 100 interviews. The students were instructed to collect the information from any adult member of the household contacted. This turned out to be 34 percent men and 66 percent women.

Tecate is not as densely populated as most Mexican cities, although it has the typical grid pattern of streets centered on the plaza, church, government buildings, and businesses. It is divided into a "primary section" and the more recent and more outlying *colonias* and *fraccionamientos*. The city has only an informal and somewhat contradictory house-numbering system, only a few street signs, all in the downtown area. House size ranged from one to nine rooms with a mean average of 4.2 rooms. The number of beds ranged from one to nine with a mean at 3.8. Values of the house and land ranged from less than $100 to over $20,000, with a mean of about $4,000 and a median of about $3,000. The few who rent pay an average of $16 a month, but their homes tend to have few facilities.

The majority own (65 percent) and have built (56 percent) their own homes. In fact, 86 percent of those who indicated that they own their homes also said that they constructed the home themselves, most of them with some or all of their own labor. House lots are generally sold in plots of 15 by 30 meters, but frequently more than one house is built on the plot. Choice of a particular site to build a house was determined primarily by the availability of inexpensive or free government land, while closeness to work, the children's school, and to the center of town were also moderately important reasons.

Aside from our survey results there are other indications—such as value of residential land—that proximity to the downtown area of the plaza, the church, and the business district is very desirable. This contrasts with the attitude in the U.S. in which locations in the hills above the town with their panoramic views and their location away from the noise and traffic is desirable. The poorest residential districts in Tecate are located on hillsides, are the farthest from the downtown area, are quieter, and have the best views. The outlying *colonias* lack paved roads or street lights, and many families raise a few farm animals, especially pigs and chickens, although there are also a few milk cows. The outlying homes are usually constructed by the owners with inexpensive materials, so they are uneven in quality.

House materials range in quality from composite materials (18 percent), unfired adobe bricks (3 percent), wood frames, often with stucco covering (21 percent), to fired brick masonry (58 percent). The houses tend to be one-story box-like structures with low-pitched roofs, cement floors, and only rough finishing in terms of painting, screens, and light fixtures. Garages are only rarely built, although carports are fairly common. The high enclosing walls found in central Mexico are uncommon in Tecate. Wooden or wire fences, a garden of cooking herbs and a few flowers, and the backyard as a cluttered trash and storage area are common features in Tecate. There is considerable heterogeneity in the value of homes in the same neighborhood, particularly in the downtown areas. Thus, we may find a mansion worth $30,000 next to a shack worth $300. One social concomitant of this is that the more economically homogeneous outlying *colonias* have greater cooperation and *esprit de corps* and are more neighborhoods in a social as well as a physical sense than the downtown areas. Outlying *colonias* tend to be more politically active than inner *colonias*, particularly through the Groupo Feminina de Colonias, while certain individuals in the inner Primera Seccion in fact have the greatest political power.

The city water system consists of two wells on the riverbed, a storage tank on a hill above the Primera Seccion, and a pipe system with water meters to some 57 percent of the houses. However, as in Tijuana the flow of water in the system is sporadic, especially in the summer months. Commercial tank trucks deliver water to private water-storage tanks, or *pilas* (30 pesos, or $2.40, per pila) for most of the houses that are not connected to the city water lines. Two of the outlying *colonias* cooperatively built their own well and water-distribution system.

The city sewer system is connected to 52 percent of the houses, while the rest use septic tanks (22 percent) or simple outhouses (26 percent). About 88 percent of the houses in the city have electric service, but this varies by area, so that some *colonias* entirely lack electricity, while in others every house in connected to the power system. A private gas company based in Tijuana services 86 percent of the households with 40-kilo butane gas tanks. Houses which do not use gas rely primarily on wood or oil stoves because of the high cost of electricity. Telephone service extends just to the Primera Seccion and eight centrally located *colonias*. In fact, there is a high correlation between proximity to the center of the city and the possession of domestic services such as piped water, sewer drainage, electricity, and telephone service.

There is a tendency for utilities and appliances possessed to fall into a unidimensional ordinal scale. Households with only one of the items listed below tend to have the first, a radio. Households with two items tend to have a radio and a gas stove, and so on down the list until we see that households with telephones have all of the items. Because a radio can be battery operated and all of the domestic gas in town comes in delivered tanks, it is possible to have both a radio and a gas stove without electrical service. The percentage of households that possessed an item was as follows:

Radio	83%	Car	59%
Gas stove	81%	Running water	57%
Refrigerator	69%	Septic or sewer	42%
Television	69%	Electric fan	39%
Washing machine	60%	Telephone	10%

Some 10 percent of the households have 24-hour water service. The other 47 percent who have running water have intermittent water service that increases in duration in the winter and declines in the summer, but is usually available in the mornings for from 15 minutes to 3 hours depending on specific position in the water system relative to the city water pump and storage tank. The median length of water service for those who have running water is one and one-half hours. Most of the homes in the downtown "primary section" have sewer service. Outside of this area they use either septic tanks or outhouses.

Years of living in Tecate for the informants ranged from a few months to 42 years, with a mean of 12.3 years and a median of 9.4 years. The historical picture of Tecate from several independent sets of data is one of moderate and steady growth. The only clear deviation from this stable pattern of growth is an influx in 1944, 1945, and 1946 when the unexpectedly large number of 15 percent of our sample of informants arrived. This sudden increase in population was perhaps due to the initial successful establishment and operation of the Tecate Brewry.

The reasons given for coming to Tecate center around work opportunities or high pay (35 percent), family connections (20 percent), the comfortable climate (16 percent), and an enjoyment of the social life in Tecate (15 percent). The importance of social activities in Tecate contrasts with the U.S. and its "Protestant" value of hard work and reticence in accepting pleasure. Publicly, Tecate has well-attended weekly amateur music nights on Thursdays and dances on Saturdays and Sundays in the plaza all summer long. Privately, a birthday, saint's name day, or a wedding is sufficient reason for a large party with dancing. At these occasions social class and kinship ties still determine who is invited. We saw no fighting or particularly obnoxious drunken behavior, but figuratively the town runs on Tecate beer. Free beer was given away at a large amateur rodeo. Every grocery store, every cafe, and every food-and-drink stall around the plaza sells beer. The brewery's display, shows, and beer stalls dominate the annual fair, Baja California en Marcha.

Household size ranged from 1 to 14, with a mean of 5.6 persons and a median of about 5 persons. Mean age for the total was 22.9 years; median, 18 years. Migration was reflected in the age patterns, so that the mean age of 31.2 percent of the population born in Tecate is younger (11.9 years) than the 15.1 percent born in Baja California (19.0 years), and both of these populations are younger than the 53.7 percent born outside Baja California (30.8 years). These figures indicate a tendency for younger men and women to come from outside the area to Baja California and to Tecate, to settle down, and then raise their families rather than come in as older people with full families. That is, migration is for the young.

The years of education of those 16 years of age and older ranged from 0 to 15 years, with a mean average of 5.6 years. Six years of primary education is compulsory today, and most of the children are going on through junior high school. The possible alternatives after junior high school are the technical high school or the college preparatory high school. Construction of a new public high school has recently stimulated even more attendance.

About one-half (48.0 percent) of our total sample was born in Baja California. Jalisco (11.6 percent), Sinaloa (8.6 percent), Sonora (8.4 percent), and Michoacan (7.7 percent) were also important as sources of the population. These states are in western Mexico and are all connected by the major communication route of Highway 15. Family connections also run north and indicate that Baja California serves as a transitional zone for migration to the U.S. We found that more of our sample had relatives in the U.S. (76 percent) than in Tecate (63 percent).

The occupations of the employed members of our sample were divided into the sectors of manufacturing (30 percent), services (30 percent), retailing (14 percent), government (13 percent), construction (7 percent), and agriculture and animal husbandry (6 percent). The industrial character of the town is clearly shown in these figures. Monthly household income ranged from $15 to $950, with a mean household income of $229, a median household income of $170, a mean per employee income of $142, and a per capita income of $40.

We found that 23 percent of our informants do not cross the border into the U.S. and another 20 percent cross less than four times a year. There are individuals in our sample who have lived in Tecate for over 15 years and have never been even to Tecate, California, which to most people is simply another part of the town. Children living along Avenida Mexico, which parallels the border, slip under the fence to play in the open fields on the U.S. side. In one place Mexican mothers push their children in a swing that hangs in an oak grove on the U.S. side. The majority of the population cross the border frequently (13 percent from 5 to 50 times a year, 14 percent "once a week," and 29 percent more than once a week) to buy things (57 percent) or to visit friends or relatives (15 percent). Some people go to the U.S. to work (5 percent) or for vacation travel (4 percent).

Of those who do go to the U.S., the median is about six times a month. The majority of these trips are to the American market or to the U.S. Post Office in Tecate, California. In order of frequency with which they are mentioned, the major foods purchased at the American market are milk, chicken, potatoes, and lard. A great number of other items such as household appliances and cars are typically purchased in the U.S. The cars in Tecate are virtually all American made. About 25 percent of the cars that are owned by people who live in Tecate have California license plates. The owners purchased used cars in California and simply kept the plates to avoid paying Mexican taxes.

Reported church attendance was very high, with some 60 percent claiming they go once a week and 16 percent claiming they go more than once a week. Counts of the number actually attending church show that the level of participation is much lower. Church designations were 88 percent Catholic, 11 percent in seven different Protestant sects, and 1 percent gave no answer. Compared to Catholics, the Protestants tend to have lower incomes and fewer household utilities, more often to live in the outlying *colonias*, to have lived in Tecate a shorter period of time, and to have a higher level of church participation. The church was found to play a more dominant role in the socialization of children among Protestants than among Catholics.

Tecate's politics were found to be heavily influenced by the state and national levels of government, by political parties, and by private associations. The current local government was not very autonomous, but was integrated and responsive to several outside agencies. Tecate's border location was found to have no direct impact on Tecate's politics, although indirect influences from the United States in the form of economic and social ties were important.

The main problems of Tecate were seen as lack of sufficient water (94 percent said this), the need for paving and improving the streets (39 percent), the need for more employment opportunities (31 percent), the need for a sewer system (21 percent), domestic electricity (20 percent), and better educational facilities (4 percent). The advantages of Tecate were seen as primarily the climate

(53 percent said this) and the character of the town (50 percent): "peaceful," "small," "quiet," "lack of crime," and "high morality."

Responses to the question "Would you like to live in the United States?" were 69 percent "Yes," 27 percent "no," and 4 percent did not answer. They tend to like the higher wages and material advantages of the U.S., but they prefer the more friendly and relaxed social patterns of life in Mexico.

A Tecate Family

The Moreno* family came from Guadalajara to Tijuana in 1957 when Sr. Moreno's construction business failed. At first they lived with relatives while Sr. Moreno tried to sell silver jewelry he had purchased before leaving Guadalajara. That business failed too. The silver had too much copper in it. He changed jobs frequently for three lean years. The family usually could not afford doctors, even for a child delivery and several serious illnesses.

Hearing of a job in the area of his ancestral home, Sr. Moreno moved the family back south to Morelia. The job did not materialize; they wanted a younger man. His relatives did little to help, and they scorned his family for the habits of poor dress and bad manners they had acquired in the north. Finally, through the help of friends, Sr. Moreno got a highway department job back in Baja California based in Tecate. The family was finally able to buy a small house near the railroad tracks. After three years in Tecate Sr. Moreno was then transferred to Ensenada, but the family had grown to six older children by now. They had a home, they liked the small city, and so they stayed in Tecate. Sr. Moreno worked in Ensenada and visited his family on weekends. In another year he had

*The names have been changed in this sketch from our 1967 study.

cancer and had to leave his job. He was bedridden for several months and then finally died.

Those hard early years drew the family close together. Now the two oldest children are working, the family operates a small store, and Sra. Moreno and her six children live a middle-class life in Tecate. When Sr. Moreno became ill, Sra. Moreno started the store in her front room to sell beans, rice, sugar, candy, and other goods to the neighborhood. A separate store was built on the property with the money from Sr. Moreno's insurance policy. Now, by keeping it open from 7:00 a.m. to 9:00 p.m. seven days a week with the help of the three boys the family nets about $110 per month from the store. They have a truck so that they can buy goods wholesale in Tijuana, but it gives the family a new mobility for other occasions as well.

Dolores is the oldest at 24, and she works as a secretary at an electronics firm in Tecate. She is sensitive about not being married by her age, but she says that in Tecate "The most desirable males—those with a better future—go away to study and never come back." "Dating has always been chaperoned in Tecate. Rarely does a girl go alone with a boy. If she does, her reputation is in danger." "We used to go to parties. Father would let us do that. But he would come and pick us up at 9:00, so what was the use of going? After awhile we stopped going."

Very few of the rich in Tecate look down on the poor. In the South the high-class people are those who have come from aristocratic families. Baja California is too young to have such a traditional social hierarchy. This is a small town, so the concept of high society is just starting to be meaningful. Here a person's merit is more important in getting ahead. The women think more for themselves. A woman should be able to work at a profession without social disapproval.

Maria is 20, and she works as a secretary near Tijuana. Maria has to get up at 6:00 a.m. every working day to catch her bus for a half-hour ride to work. In her spare time she enjoys tending her small garden in the front yard.

Elena is 19, and unlike most girls in Tecate, she is finishing high school. She spends her spare time drawing and would like to be a fashion designer. To do that "I would have to go to art school in Mexico City. At this time that would be impossible since I will have to work to help put my brothers through school."

When I was in the nun's school I was very shy. I wouldn't speak to anybody. All I did was study. It was a girl's school, so when I got into public high school I was very scared. But it was a good experience. In an all-girl's school groups of girls are always criticizing one another. They were always making such a big thing out of their boyfriends, and when I told them I didn't have one they wouldn't let me hear the end of it. It is best that boys and girls are separated so that the girls can learn to conduct themselves properly.

In high school all the girls act shy in class. The boys really play a lot. They're always making a lot of noise. They hang around in groups. The girls stay on one side of the school usually and the boys on the other. We don't like to mix. We would rather be alone because the boys are rough with us in their talk and actions.

Jorge is 17 and plays on a basketball team for his school. He says that most of the athletes in Tecate smoke and drink too much. "To prove their *macho* they'll have a cigarette before a game and one after. If they lose, they get drunk to forget the game. If they win, they get drunk to celebrate." The family is saving money so that if his grades are good enough he can go on to college in Mexico City.

Juan is 15 and Jose is 13. The three brothers spend much of their time together: taking turns running the store, playing basketball or soccer in the yard, building a clubhouse or a soap-box car, helping a younger brother with his homework, playing with the family dog, or just talking and joking. The boys all hope to go as far in school as they can. Then, when the boys finish school, the family may move to Guadalajara and stay together there where the boys could get good jobs.

A working day begins with Maria getting ready to catch

her bus. She washes with water dipped from a tank outside the house and then fixes her breakfast with eggs and cereal from the family store. Her two sisters often join her for breakfast. Dolores goes into the boy's room and wakes Juan who must open the store. Elena usually fixes breakfast for the three boys. Sra. Moreno takes it easy now that the family has grown up, mostly reading and sewing, while she takes a shift of running the store.

Elena, when she is not in school, usually stays in the house to cook and clean, or draw when she finds time. The biggest meal of the day is from 1:00 to 2:00 p.m. Dolores comes home from work and helps Elena and her mother fix it. The usual meals have meat, rice, beans, a soup, and tortillas prepared in various ways. There is always plenty of food now. Dolores says

> Mother always laughed at our poverty when father couldn't get a job. She made a joke about not having enough food, so it didn't seem so bad. One reason why I'm not anxious to get married right away is that I want a husband who will be able to support our children well—not in luxury but not in poverty as we were at one time. Many people in Tecate are in poverty today because of the low-paying jobs or lack of work.

The girls do most of the heavy household chores on Saturday mornings: sweeping and mopping the floors, gardening, and washing the clothes and bedding. The washing is done with a machine, but the water for it must be carried in from a tank, so the boys help at this. On Saturday afternoons the family usually goes to Tijuana with Jorge driving the truck. They shop for meat, clothing, or goods for the store. On Sundays the family goes to the Catholic Church in the morning, and unless there is a festival or rodeo around town, afternoons are spent around the house.

By combining the salaries of Dolores, Maria, and the income from the store, the family earns about $250 per month. This has allowed them to buy most of the modern appliances such as a gas stove, a refrigerator, and a television set. Most nights the family watches television, often programs from American stations, and sees an even higher standard of living. Dolores says, "Sometimes I envy the Americans for the beautiful things they have, yet I don't want to just buy such things from the U.S. I would like to see Mexico make them. I would like to see Mexico develop much more than it has."

Life is open-ended for the Moreno children. Hard working, determined to become educated, coordinated as a family team, they plan their future with a clear vision of obstacles and possibilities. If they ever were seemingly trapped in a culture of poverty, that old way of life is certainly over. Perhaps the Moreno family is not statistically "average," but their spirit of enterprise is characteristic of Tecate and Tijuana.

Contrasting Types of Border Cities

Tecate and Tijuana are both border cities in Baja California, but their different relationships to the United States help us to analyze the American impact on northern Mexico. Tecate has extremely little American tourism, while in Tijuana American tourists are the major source of income. For example, in fiscal 1967 only 1.7 percent of the 14 million U.S. citizen entries along the California border came over at the Tecate border station, while 74.0 percent entered from the Tijuana-San Ysidro station (U.S. Immigration and Naturalization Service, 1968). Both cities are, in per capita terms, among the most prosperous cities in Mexico.

Like many cities of northern Mexico, Tecate began as a ranching center, but its location spurred it on to city status. Although it was too far from San Diego for significant tourist traffic, the town's industries reflected the export market and sales to tourists in other border towns. Factories for the manufacture of malt, whisky, wine, and beer were established. Tecate participated in the economic boom brought to Ensénada, Tijuana, and Mexicali during the Prohibition era without itself being inundated by American tourists. Tecate developed a reputation as a good place to raise children, and the people began actively to promote that reputation. Even the establishment of the city's two souvenir shops was resisted, because "We don't want the vice that tourism generates and we don't want to be servants to the Americans." A large resort and gambling casino was burned down in Tecate before it was completed, possibly as an act of local protest.

Since the end of Prohibition in the U.S. Tecate moved away from the manufacture of alcoholic beverages for the American tourist trade toward manufacturing generally, with exports to the American market continuing to play a role. Cuauhtemoc Brewery bought out the malt and beer factories in 1954 to make Tecate and Carta Blanca brands of beer. Then in 1961 a coffee-milling plant (Cafetelera Nacional), a food-packing plant (Los Mochis, subsidiary of Heinz), and a foundry were established. In recent years three small electronics assembly plants went into operation on a dual-plant basis with American firms. American capital was very important in Baja California until about 1935 and then declined almost to insignificance until dual plants began in the late 1960s.

Ensenada, Tijuana, and Mexicali are far larger cities than Tecate and thus have much more manufacturing than Tecate. Ensenada relies on tourism, the commerce of a deep seaport, fishing, and wine making; Tijuana caters to tourism and industrial production related to tourism such as the manufacturing for export of furniture, glassware, onyxware, plaster statuary, and so on; and Mexicali centers on the commerce of an agricultural region with packing, canning, and cotton ginning. Manufacturing is simply more of a predominant occupation in Tecate than in these other cities, with the brewery dominating the local scene. Tecate has very pure water in a moderate quantity, but the brewery produces from about 50,000 to 80,000 gallons of beer a day and thus preempts much of the local water from their own deep wells. Given the local political power of the brewery, it would be virtually impossible for new water-using industries to locate in Tecate. However, new electronics assembly plants and other similar industries may very well locate there.

The strong economic viability of Tecate and its relative independence from the tourist trade have promoted a strong local pride in Tecate. The Junta de Mejoramiento, or Civic Improvement League, actively promotes Mexican traditions and ensures that all Mexican national holidays are observed. Competitive athletic teams in soccer, volleyball, and basketball represent the city, which also participates in an annual cross-country bicycle race. Although people complain of insufficient water, paving, employment, the sewer system, and domestic electrical connections, they are still enthusiastic about the advantages of Tecate over other places in the U.S. and Mexico. They like the climate and the peaceful prosperity of Tecate, which they see as lacking in crime, high in morality, and a good place to raise children.

Tijuana is far larger and more heterogeneous city than Tecate. Its history is from ranch, to ranching town, to way station and tourist shop between Ensenada and San Diego, to a major tourist attraction in its own right, and finally to a diversified city. Tijuana has had a recent high population growth due to a prosperity induced by massive increases in the number of tourists coming down from California. Tijuana is a specialized kind of city that virtually lacks natural resources. It is specialized in selling services to American tourists, and this is possible because the wage level is lower in Mexico than it is in the U.S. If the U.S.-Mexico border was closed (as has happened occasionally in the past) all the other cities of Baja California except Tijuana would continue to have a moderate level of prosperity. But Tijuana would be extremely hurt by a permanent closing of the border. Tijuana's location at the border is central to its reason for being. The existence of Tijuana is dependent on the present kind of semipermeable border where a certain limited flow of goods and people is allowed. Ciudad Juarez has a similar symbiotic character, but Tecate, Mexicali, and certain other border cities are more autonomous.

The quality of life is quite different in Tecate and Tijuana. The personalism that pervades Tecate's "primary community" social relations contrasts with Tijuana's impersonalism, present even in many of Tijuana's residential suburbs such as Colonia Libertad. We found that the people of Libertad largely lacked the sense of community that we found in Tecate. There are 131 named districts in Tijuana, and the varying characters of these districts cover an extremely wide range, from squatters' shacks to upper-class mansions, from recent immigrants to founding families. Most are so new as to lack piped water, sewer drainage, or paved streets. Some still lack even electricity. Tijuana's diversity is also a product of the diverse backgrounds of the Tijuanese, immigrants mostly from the states of western Mexico. All of the household heads interviewed in Colonia Libertad had come as immigrants to Tijuana.

Tijuana, like all major border cities, has separate districts for tourists and regular commerce. The mutual social isolation of Americans and Mexicans has developed perhaps more completely in Tijuana than other border cities because the pressures for tourist intrusions into private lives are greater with such a high volume of tourist traffic. Still, despite this social isolation Tijuana is influenced by American culture. For example, Tijuana has a small teenage subculture that wears "mod" clothing, listens to "rock" music, and does the "twist" dances. By contrast, Tecate's summer social events in the city plaza draw people from every age group and every social strata. In Tecate people of all ages go to the same dances, and they do traditional dances like the waltz and fox-trot. In Tecate the social classes are less insulated from each other.

The different levels of urbanization between Tecate and Tijuana are probably the major determinants in their different styles of life, but the stronger American influence also seems to give Tijuana certain qualities that are lacking in Tecate. Ultimately both cities are heavily dependent on commerce with Americans. They are also involved in a symbiotic relationship with the United States that goes beyond economics to kinship ties, ideological ties, and so on. However, Tecate's relationship in this symbiosis is so indirect that it has been able to develop along more traditional lines.

viii: *The International Border as a Cultural Context for Urbanization*

The Heterogenetic Frontier

Tijuana developed away from the heartland of Mexico, in a different kind of physical environment and in closer contact with the United States than most Mexican cities. It developed where Anglo and Hispanic traditions meet in the New World and thus has borrowed and reinterpreted parts of Anglo and United States culture. The birth from mixed sources of origin we see here is the creation of original modes of culture, whether by changing to fit new environments or by influence from other cultures. Not only do we find that Mexicans have immigrated to this northern frontier and changed their culture to fit a new land and new neighboring culture but the same frontier has attracted Chinese, East Indians, Russians, Frenchmen, Englishmen, and others in search of freedom and opportunity. The Chinese were at one time the most populous ethnic group in the Mexicali Valley, as tenant farmers for American landlords. Ensenada was initially developed by an American and then an English land-development company. The mining booms in Baja California brought down hundreds of Americans from California. The Little Landers were a cooperative agricultural group that settled early in the San Ysidro area, across the border from Tijuana.

The history of the frontier area is filled with cases of

pioneers, communal settlements, and utopian communities. The Mexican national *ejido*, or commune program, has been successful in many places in the north, such as the Mexicali Valley and the Ensenada area. On a smaller scale we find that close to Tecate there is a yoga institute headed by a prominent Hindu yoga, Indra Devi. She has a fairly large estate with a dormitory for students, a dining hall, and rooms for exercise and contemplation.

Just down the road from the yoga institute is Rancho La Puerta, a "European Styled Health Spa." Although a commercial operation today, it began as a utopian commune of health enthusiasts who believed in maintaining "a perfect balance between physical and spiritual health." Edmond Szekely was in the Pacific, the United States, and then Mexico writing for French and English health magazines when war was stirring in Europe in the late 1930s. In 1940 he decided not to go back to Europe, but instead went to Tecate and set up a communal farm called Academia de Filosofia "La Puerta" Sociedad de Estudios Comparativos de Culturas Antiguas. Members of the commune were recruited through the health magazines to leave strife-torn Europe and come to a beautiful ranch in the Mediterranean climate of Tecate. The students came, set up tents, farmed, and attended lectures in the open air.

Over the years more permanent facilities were constructed, and observers were invited to visit the ranch. Those who came for short stays tended to be more interested in the physical than the philosophical aspects of the academy's program, and with an increase in visitors the program shifted toward physical exercise and dieting. The ranch makes its own whole wheat bread and produces wild sage honey. The juice of local grapes is always on tap and is used in a French "grape cure" for various medical problems, and the ranch serves vegetarian meals made from its own organically grown fruits and vegetables. Where once the Mexicans of Tecate thought of Rancho La Puerta as a bizarre nudist colony, today they simply refer to it as an "American fat farm." Rancho La Puerta has become a dieter's resort with swimming pools, a gymnasium, and the usual facilities for massages, steam baths, and facials.

The Russians of Guadalupe

Another idealistic community was the Russian Colony of Guadalupe Valley, between Tecate and Ensenada (Dewey, 1966 and Schmieder, 1928). The Molokanye, a persecuted religious sect from the plains of Southern Russia, were forced to move to Kars in the Armenian highlands of Southern U.S.S.R. Then in the late 1800s they immigrated to Canada, the U.S.A., Mexico, and other New World areas for freedom to practice their religion and to avoid the economic and military draft problems that preceded the Russian Revolution of 1905. The Molokanye were conscientious objectors to participation in war who, because of their antiwar stand, were deprived of their farms. Some were exiled to Siberia before their general exodus began. Their emigration was opposed by the Russian government, so they were forced to leave in small groups. The colonies in San Francisco and Los Angeles became particularly large and important ones, but many of the people feared that their way of life would be heavily influenced by American culture, and they found that the high land prices of California prevented them from taking over large tracts of land to cultivate cooperatively in their traditional way. Northern Baja California attracted them because the climate was similar to southern California, while the land was cheaper and the population of Baja was so small they could employ their traditional form of agriculture and have more control over their own children.

In 1905 two delegates from the Los Angeles community were sent to Baja California to locate a permanent agricultural settlement for the sect. They selected the 13,014 acre ranch of Ex-Mission Guadalupe 22 miles northeast of Ensenada. The original price of $50,000 was high for that time, but 100 families came to farm and they turned over half of their crops to the community for payments, so that the ranch was paid for in only a few years. The Molokanye were granted permission to become citizens of Mexico, and in 1906 they received official guarantees of religious freedom and a suspension of customs duties for the Molokan colony.

The colony was operated according to the Russian *mir* system, used in Russia since the fifteenth century, in which the land belongs to the parish and each family receives the right to use lots for a house and a garden within the village and for field crops and pasture outside the village. After the fall harvest all fields become common grazing pasture until spring planting. Taxes were collected within the colony by a village elder. The geographic plan of the village was the East European *strassendorf:* one long street with homes, barns, and garden plots located on each side rather than the Latin American form of a central plaza with outlying farms. Each family received approximately two acres of land in the village for their house, a barn, poultry pens, a garden, and an orchard. The houses were built of adobe with the Russian hipped roof, first of thatch and then later of redwood shingles from the United States.

Family life was strongly patriarchal and marked by marriage only to other Molokanye. Postmarital residence was patrilocal until all expenses incurred during the wedding were paid, which might take three or four years. There were customs such as cleaning the house and taking a steam bath in the backyard on Saturdays, no use of tobacco, drinking alcoholic beverages only at weddings and fiestas, and avoidance of modern influence, such as the telephone and movies.

Foods were primarily tea, *borscht* soups, black bread, cheese, stewed poultry, and beef. They had a food taboo on pork and were initially resistant to the eating of fish, lobster, or clams. Every household was largely self-sufficient with little specialization within the community, each household producing most of the things it needed from candles to clothing.

Women wore blouses and long, gathered skirts of shoe-top length, usually worn with a white apron. When visiting or at church the women were proud of the lace shawls they wore over their heads. Men wore a visored cap, a high-collared *moujik* blouse, and baggy overalls tucked into calf-high boots. Older men wore full beards. The blouse of the husband and the wife's skirt were always the same color, forming a family color. Sometimes the fence or other features were painted in the same color. Russian-style steam baths were built near the homes.

The Molokan ("milk-eater"; they drank milk during Lent) religion began in the seventeenth century by breaking off from the Russian-Greek Orthodox Church. It rejected icons, the trinitarian doctrine, sainthood, an ordained and paid priesthood, and sacraments; forbade oath taking and the bearing of arms; and integrated the church with political and economic life. They thus sought an area with enough religious freedom to allow them to create a small, internal theocracy. Their religious service was usually held in the homes and involved about three hours of reading from the scripture, singing in choral harmony, a financial collection, a group prayer, and a brotherly kiss of elders and then each other. A feast and a discussion of the problems of the colony followed the religious ceremony. They were self-governing and had no police or formal courts, but the Mexican government sent teachers and required their children between 6 and 14 to attend school to learn Spanish and the basics of education. Russian continued to be spoken in church and in the home.

In 1937 an *ejido* was established next to the Russian colony and helped to foster its dissolution. The Molokanye soon realized that *ejidos* were often formed out of large, privately owned estates like the colony. They also realized the antiforeign sentiments in the Mexican Revolution, so that even though they were Mexican citizens they were often discriminated against as foreigners. The fear that their land would be seized and turned into an *ejido* led the colony after 1947 to divide the property into 49 privately owned parcels with separate legal titles. Then some of the

Russians began to move away and sell their land, first to Russians and then to non-Russians.

By 1965 only 34 percent of the arable land in the original colony was still owned by people with some Russian ancestry. The breakup was particularly speeded up by the invasion of the Russian land by squatters. In 1958 some 3,000 squatters led by Braulio Maldonado came to Guadalupe Valley from Mexicali, overrunning Russian land and setting up cardboard shacks on the theory that any currently unused land was automatically open for settlement. Maldonado became governor, and he refused to send in state troops. The Russians were successful in getting federal troops to evict all but about 300 squatters, but more squatters came in 1959, and although the federal troops tried again, most of them refused to leave. Fear for their personal safety and their property, the uncertainty of a future for the colony in Mexico, and the insecurity of absentee ownership led most of the Russians to sell off their farms. Today the squatters' homes are interspersed among the older Russian ones, and food and dress in the valley are almost entirely Mexican. The Russian church has been closed for several years, there are no more Russian festivals, and the only marked continuities are the remaining Russian-type houses and the blond and blue-eyed features of some of the valley's residents. Most of the younger Russians have moved back to rejoin the large Molokan community in Los Angeles. The few older Russians left reminisce about the early colony, complain about the squatters, and get along well with the *ejido* Mexicans, who they say cooperate with each other and respect the rights of others. While some 100 Russian families came in 1905 and there were still 45 families in 1938, there were only 7 Russian families (23 people) left in 1968.

Cultural Adaptation

Cultural adaptation is an evolutionary, temporal concept that covers such processes as transculturation (cultural change as a result of the meeting of different cultural systems), assimilation (progressive integration or incorporation of two social systems), and adjustment (social and psychological health).

The California-Baja California border did not develop as a significant cultural phenomenon until 1917. The movement of people and goods across the border was relatively free until then, and Mexican culture graded gradually into American culture. Now the transition is more abrupt, but there is still a zone of third culture along both sides of the border which is a syncretization of Mexican and American cultures. Kinship ties link people on both sides of the border. The currency of both countries is accepted on both sides of the border in regular retail stores. Spanish or English is widely spoken as a second language in this zone. There is a transculturation of foods, architecture, dress, and many other customs in both directions across the border.

While cultural adaptation is a two-way street in this case, with Mexican culture and society having an impact on America, the fact that America is the economically dominant partner predisposes that Mexican culture will change more than American culture and that Mexicans will generally be forced into socially subordinate roles vis-à-vis Americans. This inequality is the basis for much of the stress and poor adjustment (that is, poor social and psychological health) in the symbiosis. The crime rate in Tijuana appears to be partially correlated with this adaptive stress and appears to be declining as the two economic systems approach equality. There appears to be a progressive decline in the per capita crime rate since the 1940s, in spite of the tremendous increase in the size of the city, a factor that is generally correlated with a rising crime rate.

One of the greatest laboratories for the study of cultural adaption is the rapidly growing city because decades may produce significant adaptive cultural shifts. Tijuana is changing so fast that the Tijuanese are filled with the sense of change, excited by their possibilities. By drawing on

American affluence, the population has been more than doubling each decade for the last three decades. New arts, new crafts, new services, and new industries are everywhere in evidence. The Tijuanese are creative in language, and neologisms that defy a traditional Spanish dictionary flourish in their speech (*yonke* is "junk," for example). The city has received migrants from all of Mexico, so that a greater racial diversity and an acceptance of that diversity is evident.

While the sentiment exists that borrowing degrades the purity of pristine cultures, the historical fact is that the most incorporative cultures have been the most creative and most adaptive in the sense of survival and growth. American culture has been extremely incorporative, for example, its language borrowing from all the world. Tijuana borrows heavily from American culture, and the process of incorporation produces, not an American culture in Mexico, but a third and unique culture by the syncretic combination of American and Mexican elements. It is in this sense of cultural creativity that Tijuana's location at the border of Mexico, its frontier traditions, its recently arrived and diverse population, its hosting of millions of Americans annually, and its transitional position between the large Mexican-American population of California and the mainland Mexicans are all major factors in its cultural adaptation. The postindustrial Americans find recreation and an interesting and contrasting culture in Tijuana, while the Tijuanese acquire wealth so necessary for capital investments in their drive for industrialization. This is the framework of Mexican border culture within which an explanation of a city like Tijuana must lie.

Urbanization in the Context of an International Border

Three major cultural dynamics come together in modern Baja California: urbanization, the dynamics of a frontier culture, and the cultural dynamics that take place at an international border. In urbanization people have been dislocated from traditional peasant and largely self-sufficient communities and drawn into a labor market. They then move in response to the changing market conditions of an industrialization that draws great numbers of people into the cities. In this context people have been attracted to Baja California by the promise of better jobs and cheap or free land. There are *ejidos* in every agricultural valley, and over 40,000 city lots had been given away by 1958. While Mexican land reform has its roots in a democracy rejecting feudal land tenure, it was stimulated in Baja California through a nationalistic rejection of foreign control of the land. Both foreign interests and nationalism seem to thrive in frontiers generally, whether in the historic American West or Baja California. The people of Baja California seem very nationalistic, even today with frontier culture fading fast. The land probably fell under foreign control in the first place because it was isolated from mainland Mexico and it contained few natural resources, the same reasons that make it a frontier rather than an early center of growth.

Baja California has at least three kinds of frontiers. One is the classical frontier with its struggling pioneers who have displaced the aborigines and are trying to wrest a subsistence from substantially free land in an area where there is a low man-land ratio. Another frontier is Baja California as an outer fringe of Mexico, geographically and culturally, with relatively low integration with the rest of Mexico. And, finally, the major cities of northern Baja California are participating in the innovative frontier of Mexican industrialization and urbanization. Baja California differs from the classical western American frontier in that it lacks abundant natural resources. In the past it has continued as a frontier more out of its poverty than its abundance.

The classic frontier pressures for democracy have effected many changes on immigrants into Baja California. A rugged individualism and self-sufficiency tempered by a ready willingness to help neighbors and even strangers in need is characteristic of Baja California, particularly in the country. Even in the northern cities it seems that frontier characteristics have forced the weakening of the ascriptive social classes. Mexicans talk of Baja California as a frontier. It is not *really* Mexico, but it is a place of opportunity. The separation of the people of Baja California from the heartland of Mexican culture and the ever-present contrasts that Mexican culture has with American culture make these Mexicans more conscious of their Mexican heritage and more patriotic about it than in Mexico generally. Fine arts, literature, and the social niceties are blunted. It has a more lawless character where the squatter, the gambler, and the able opportunist can flourish. It is a hard life, but the rewards and the freedom from controls are greater.

The California-Baja California border did not develop as a significant cultural phenomenon until the early 1900s. The movement of people and goods across the border was relatively free until then, and Mexican culture graded gradually into American culture. Now the transition is more abrupt. However, currency of both countries is accepted on both sides. Spanish or English is widely spoken as a second language in this zone. There is a transculturation of foods, architecture, dress, and many other customs in both directions across the border. Also, institutions have developed to facilitate a compromise between conflicting national interests and to handle the flow of goods and people across the border: government agents for immigration, customs, health, and police activities and such private agents as customs experts and immigration attorneys.

When all these elements of urbanization, frontier, and border are mixed in the same social setting we should not be surprised to find great social problems, but we also find important innovations. The spirit of social revolution is fostered in the frontier cultural climate of Baja California. The definition of what is the essence of Mexican culture and identity is worked out in the give-and-take with Americans. Out of this ferment of social change we can expect the border areas to make significant contributions to modern Mexican culture.

ix: *Boundary Marking,* *Screening, and Smuggling*

The social sciences have generally focused on aspects of single societies or nations rather than on the cultural mechanisms that develop to relate and mediate between societies. Warfare, intersocietal trade and migration, and the establishment and protection of borders are perennial problems that we know very little about, largely because they are intersocietal in character.

Cultures along borders are influenced by the fact that they are at the physical frontier of a political entity. Thus, for example, border cities are usually not selected as national or state capitals due to such factors as the greater convenience of transportation from various outlying areas to a more central point and fear of foreign cultural influences or even military attack. Border cultures are also influenced by adopting cultural traits from foreign cultures, by providing goods and services for foreign visitors that are too expensive or illegal in the foreign country, and by operating or eluding the government's national screens on flows across the border.

If a border is permeable or passable and the cultures on the two sides of the border are different, then each side will serve as a special market for the other side. Within the communities along the border, institutions and cultural traditions also often develop that are designed to facilitate the movement of goods and people across the border:

customs brokers and migration lawyers at the legal level
and counterfeiters and smugglers at the illegal level.

International borders become complex cultural institutions that evolve out of international relations, out of the
needs to promote and protect nations by controlling the
flows of people, goods, and diseases across their borders.
The border is crucial to the definition of the nation state
so that the less control there is of these flows the more
integrated neighboring nation states will become, while the
restraint of flows is crucial to the definition of a border.
Without the restraint of flows there is a *formal border* but
no *effective border*. Language and cultural differences contribute to the separation of nations and the subsequent
strengthening of the control of flows at their common
border. Thus, there is less of an effective international
border, less restraint on flows, between the U.S. and Canada than there is between the U.S. and Mexico.

Canada and the U.S. *monitor* (inspect) international
flows at about the same level, but there is little *screening*
(restraint) of the flows. People migrate back and forth
with relative ease, and reciprocal trade agreements are
liberal. Each is the other's best international trading partner. Each has a common history of having been a colony
of the British Empire, and now each is an industrialized
country with a relatively low population density and vast
resources. Canada and the U.S. are so culturally close and
economically symbiotic—dissimilar in many respects, yet
living in a mutually beneficial relationship—that it has been
hypothesized that the two countries are evolving into a
single nation-state. Canadian national sentiments are extremely opposed to such a drift or evolution, so much so
that the daily press in Canada is filled with articles attack-
ing U.S. economic and cultural imperialism in Canada.
However, no one even suggests such an integration between the U.S. and Mexico; it is almost inconceivable.

Following the Mexican Revolution of 1910 many safe-
guards were built into the Mexican Constitution and legal
system against foreign influences. Foreigners cannot own

land in Mexico within 100 kilometers from an international border or 50 kilometers from a seacoast. Mexicans must have the controlling interest (51 percent or more) in corporations based in Mexico. In late 1972 President Luis Echeverria signed a decree requiring factories that make automobile spare parts to be 60 percent Mexican owned. Religious missionaries must be Mexican citizens to proselytize in Mexico. Tariffs on automobiles, home appliances, and many other goods imported into Mexico are very high. While the oil industry was at one time owned and operated by foreign interests, it has now been nationalized and is operated by a government monopoly, Pemex.

This national stance has meant that foreign investment in Mexico is relatively small ($3.5 billion) at a time when Mexico is industrializing and in great need of capital. Thus, only 3 percent of U.S. direct foreign investment is in Mexico (U.S. Bureau of Census, 1972), but this still constitutes about 80 percent of Mexico's total foreign investment. Mexico is clearly proud of the progress that it is making on its own. Also, a few years ago Mexico worked out a legal arrangement to facilitate the operation of dual-plant industries along its northern border that are taxed only on a "value-added" basis. This is promoting the rapid industrialization of such cities as Tijuana, Mexicali, and Juarez with hundreds of new plants in such labor intensive operations as television assembly and the manufacture of clothing. The urbanization of Tijuana is thus directly stimulated by its proximity to U.S. markets.

Boundary Marking

It is useful to bring together three cultural processes that typically occur in relation to the border itself, specifically *boundary marking*, *screening*, and *smuggling*. Boundary marking is the physical location of the border between two geopolitical entities on maps and on the ground. This appears to be related to such phenomena as the general human designs of territoriality, as the structural needs in legally based state societies to have explicit understandings about the areal jurisdictions of laws and policing agencies, and as a common political solution to the competitive pressures for growth in neighboring societies. Also, borders in the context of state societies are a radically different kind of thing than they are in the context of band, tribal, and chiefdom societies. The extent of boundary marking reflects the need to control flows between two political entities, so that marking, symbiosis, and screening are all related. Borders can also be seen quantitatively in these terms. There is more or less marking, symbiosis, and screening in one border area than another border area, and more or less of a border.

The original U.S.-Mexico line set by the Treaty of Guadalupe Hidalgo was made in terms of *marine* features from easily located points on maps: one marine league south of the southernmost point of San Diego Bay, the middle of the Gila River where it flows into the Colorado River, and the Rio Grande. This was the initial *map marking*. Then *land marking* was achieved by surveying and placing concrete monuments, fences, and border stations along the line. The fences and stations both *mark* and *screen*. That is, they indicate the location of the border and they keep people, goods, and diseases out of the country.

A consistent feature of geopolitical borders is that in time they become precisely defined down to a terminating line, or a *verge*, rather than a *margin* with width. However, margins are used administratively. There is a margin that is used for military defense between North Korea and South Korea. The "ports of trade" like West Berlin and Hong Kong are essentially foreign enclaves that are allowed to operate within national margins because of the strategic symbiotic role they play. Berlin is so deep into the nation of East Germany that it presents continuing problems to the two countries. Hong Kong, however, is at the physical border of China, a verge defined largely by the Pacific Ocean. A verge that is defined by such a natural separator as an ocean is more stable and less of a problem in international affairs. The American base at Guantanamo on the coast of Cuba is a very unusual border arrangement because islands tend to be completely under one nation or another.

On the land there are natural features, such as mountains or rivers, that form natural barriers and thus are used as naturally "screening" borders. One problem here, however, is that cultures change, so that what is a natural barrier or division for a culture at one time may no longer be a natural barrier at a later time. The Sonoran Desert was a natural barrier and thus a useful dividing area between the U.S. and Mexico at the time of the Treaty of Guadalupe Hidalgo, but of course it is easily crossed today.

International Border Screening

Screening is control of the flows of people, goods, and diseases between geopolitical entities. Government agencies are created to carry out screening processes involving immigration and naturalization, customs, and public health. Each screening agency has a staff and specialized methods to control the flows. While the pressure for flows usually arises out of economic symbiosis, screening is usually a political design to protect a country by limiting the operation of a free competitive market. It is essentially a political process that is used to control an economic process. One cross-cultural screening technique is to force the flows to be funneled down to a limited number of inspection points at border stations, airports, and seaports. Since inspection by special police agencies is their primary function, the border stations have a neutral, or "no-man's-land," quality.

Outward Versus Inward Flows

The *outward* flows are usually not very important to a nation, so they are rarely screened. However, a nation may restrict outward flows of armaments to prevent the escalation of foreign wars. Through reciprocal agreements nations may maintain export quotas to protect foreign industries. They may keep people from leaving the country to prevent losing their skills or to prosecute criminals. Turkey, Greece, and Mexico have been particularly concerned about the illegal export of archaeological antiquities from their countries in the past several years.

Most national screens are designed to control the movements of people and goods *into* the country. There are screens that are applied to fruits, vegetables, meats, and people to prevent the importation of *diseases*. The screens of *people*, per se, are meant to protect the labor markets from an oversupply and overcompetition; to prevent the overburdening of welfare agencies, schools, and other social services; and to keep out undesirables, such as criminals, narcotic addicts, and political enemies. The screens of *goods* are meant to protect local industries from international competition, to acquire revenues through tariffs on imports, to prevent the importation of dangerous substances such as narcotics, and to prevent the excessive importation of luxuries which do not contribute to economic growth.

Screens for Diseases and Persons

Smuggling penetrates all three types of screens: diseases, persons, and goods. The disease screen is the least important, so that many countries do not have an effective one. Where a disease screen does exist, the health agency usually has a small staff, perhaps only a medical doctor and a food inspector at the major border stations. On the U.S.-Mexico border, medical inspections are required for immigrants into either country, but not for ordinary tourist visiting. The U.S. disease screens on imports are very light on vegetables, moderate on fruits, and heavy on meats. Live animals receive a particularly careful inspection, often including a period of quarantined inspection.

The screens of people are the most complicated and

carefully policed screens. Immigration, naturalization, border station inspection, and border patrol agencies operate the screens. Illegal emigration or immigration generally can be considered as a kind of smuggling, but this is usually the amateur practice of people smuggling themselves out of or into countries. Politically motivated illegal migration tends to be widely publicized, but it is not nearly as important in terms of numbers of migrants as economically motivated migration. Most of the smuggling of people operates in response to the market principles of changing supplies, demands, and prices for labor. For example, Italians today seem to migrate to Germany, France, or Canada primarily for the higher wages they can earn in these countries. They are still sentimentally attached to Italy and Italian culture, but the material rewards they can acquire through migration are more important to them. Koreans migrate to Japan and Mexicans migrate to the U.S. in much the same kind of pattern. These migrations are signs of the growth of an international labor market.

Economic disparities between nations of the world promote migrations, and these in turn tend to equalize slightly those disparities. The prosperous nations, however, are too protective of their economies to allow much of a change in the disparities. The prosperous nations create protective screens through quotas, standards, and bureaucratic red tape on the immigrants they will accept. However, when the disparities are great, they invariably receive illegal immigrants.

Illegal immigration from Mexico into the U.S. is probably the largest between any two countries in the world. In fiscal year 1969 the U.S. Border Patrol apprehended 172,391 deportable aliens, 159,395 in the Southwest Region (Seitz, 1970: 39). About 100 illegal entrants per day are arrested in the greater San Diego area alone. It is estimated that only about 3 percent of the illegal entrants elude the U.S. Immigration Service for over one year. Most of these people entered the U.S. on their own, without transportation aid from friends, relatives, or commercial smugglers. However, 2,049 smugglers and 11,784 smuggled aliens were apprehended by the U.S. Border Patrol in 1969 (fiscal). Over 92 percent of the smugglers were arrested in the Southwest Region. Additionally in 1969 (fiscal) 3,756 aliens were caught trying to enter the U.S. with altered or counterfeit documents or by using the documents of other people, and 1,221 were caught trying to enter by falsely claiming U.S. citizenship.

The commercial smuggling of Mexicans into the U.S. has markedly increased in the last several years. The smugglers' fees have risen, more professional criminals are involved, and more sophisticated planning and equipment are being used. Commercial smugglers now commonly send out additional vehicles ahead of their loads to scout for Border Patrol checkpoints and roving patrols. When a checkpoint is spotted the aliens are let out and given instructions on how to walk around the checkpoint to a place where they will be picked up again. The Border Patrol pays particular attention when a truck comes through with a large amount of personal baggage. Baggage is often left in the truck so that those walking will avoid suspicion when circling a check point. Small campers, vans, and trucks are frequently used instead of the more obvious large vans. Specially built compartmented vehicles are also used. Most of the vehicles are equipped with load-leveling devices to conceal the added weight of their passengers.

In a 1970 San Diego-Tijuana survey of attitudes toward illegal entrants into the U.S. we received no strong antiwetback comments of any kind. U.S. Border Patrolmen were very similar to the Tijuanese in their attitudes, and both were more accepting than our non-Spanish speaking respondents. One typical response of a Border Patrolman was, "The average wetback desires to work, which is a quality lacking among too many citizens of this country. He comes with the intent of hard work and is only trying to better the living conditions of himself or his family in Mexico."

The San Ysidro-Tijuana Border Station

To give an example of a large border station, the screening agencies that regularly operate at or in the vicinity of the San Ysidro Border Station are as follows: 1) U.S. Customs Service, 2) U.S. Immigration and Naturalization Service, 3) U.S. Border Patrol (an agency of I.N.S.), 4) U.S. Public Health Service, 5) U.S. Department of Agriculture, 6) U.S. Bureau of Narcotics and Dangerous Drugs, 7) U.S. Navy Shore Patrol, 8) California State Fish and Game Commission, 9) California State Department of Agriculture, and 10) San Diego Municipal Police.

Customs (5 supervisors and 35 inspectors and assistants in 1968) enforces the regulations on imports and exports, records and collects duties on this trade, and combats smuggling. The Bureau of Narcotics and Dangerous Drugs works with the Customs agents in policing the drug trade. Immigration (6 supervisors and 37 inspectors and assistants) supervises 44 different categories of aliens, involving such factors as whether they intend to immigrate or not; whether they will be tourists, or students, or diplomats, or representatives of newsmedia; and so on.

The San Diego Municipal Police Department (three or more patrolmen maintains a checkpoint for traffic leaving the city (and simultaneously leaving the U.S.). They are legally authorized to prevent persons under 18 years of age from leaving the city at this point who are not accompanied by a parent or guardian or do not have written permission to do so from their parents. Additionally, they intercept stolen cars and fugitives, check cars for safety defects, and make arrests for possession of small amounts of drugs when these are detected by U.S. Customs. Thus, the agencies cooperate to circumvent making arrests under the more severe federal laws about drug smuggling when the persons have smuggled in only small amounts of drugs for their personal use. The U.S. Highway Patrol assists with traffic problems and cooperates with the San Diego Police and U.S. Customs in apprehending suspects away from the immediate border area. The Shore Patrol has an entrance checkpoint to apprehend servicemen referred to them by the other border agencies. Border Patrolmen search areas along the international line by foot, jeep, and aircraft for the illegal entrance of aliens and livestock and for smuggling. The California State Fish and Game Commission works with Customs on weekends to spot any importation of game animals that would violate California game laws.

The U.S. Public Health Service (2 supervisors, 2 medical advisors, 12 inspectors, 1 X-ray technician, and 1 clerk) attempts to prevent the introduction of communicable diseases into the United States, including diseases that are carried by animals and are communicable to man. The Health Service also provides medical examinations for immigrants for I.N.S. There is a Department of Animal Inspection that inspects imported and exported animals and animal by-products for contagious diseases. The American race horses used at the Agua Caliente track in Tijuana, for example, are inspected by this department. The U.S. Department of Agriculture works to prevent the introduction of plant pests, such as the Mexican fruit fly, into the U.S. by inspecting incoming baggage and cargo and by sponsoring pest eradication work in northern Mexico. The California State Department of Agriculture examines imported produce for compliance with quality control and fair-packaging regulations.

While there are many border agencies, they operate cooperatively as specialized parts of a single screening process. Thus, when an individual enters the U.S. by driving a car up to a primary inspection point at a U.S. border stagion, he will be inspected by one inspector (usually employed by Customs or Immigration) who screens for customs, immigration, health, and agricultural violations. The inspector usually asks the citizenship of the people in the car and what they purchased in Mexico. If the inspector at the "primary" station suspects that something is wrong, he will mark a "Multiple Inspection Referral" form, place it under the windshield wiper of the car, and ask the driver to drive into a "secondary" inspection point. In "secondary" a specialized agent will more thoroughly investigate the suspected violation.

Mexican border officials are much less concerned with screening, and the inspectors simply wave most of the traffic through. Officials from both Customs (Aduana) and Immigration (Migracion) stand by the passing traffic at both the vehicle and pedestrian crossing points instead of using a single individual for multiple screening. Trucks, however, are consistently stopped and inspected for commercial quantities of foods, such as lard, and household appliances.

Smuggling

To smuggle (from the Lower German *smuggelin*) is to move something secretly and illegally from one political entity (such as a state, province, or nation) to another political entity. If trade were entirely free from government taxation or border traffic screening, then by definition there would be no smuggling. Smuggling is the illegal penetration of border screens. Smuggling as a crime comes, not out of common law, but out of statute laws, those created by a legislative body. It is a crime against the state rather than against persons or their personal property. Smuggling is also unique to the "state" type of societies because simpler forms of societies simply lack the kind of corporate and legal expression of societal self-interest to build legal barriers against the flow of goods. In fact, these barriers help to define the *territorial* and *legal* nature of the state society itself.

Administered Smuggling of Goods

Governments that have predominantly administered economies, mostly communist today, have had to create government agencies to smuggle restricted goods out of capitalist countries because market processes have not been able to handle this trade. Thus, for many years Communist China imported strategic goods such as steel plates, machine tools, industrical chemicals, and electronic equipment up the Pearl River into Canton through its own firms in Macao. East Germany also set up "companies" to smuggle in goods that were being restricted from Eastern trade by Western governments. The Western press played this smuggling up as an evil dimension of communist societies, but since communist societies have primarily administered rather than market economies, their action was precisely what should be expected.

While governments are not pleased by it, smuggling thrives on war and repressive trade restrictions. For example, it is illegal in wartime to export certain strategic goods, particularly to enemy countries. These laws are sometimes circumvented by going through a third, neutral country or a free port, resulting in essential trade between the enemy countries. Neutral countries play a valuable intermediary role, particularly in wartime. Wartime expenses require new sources of revenue, and these are often raised through customs and luxury taxes on goods, thus inviting smuggling that will circumvent the taxes. War calls for rationing and produces shortages in certain materials, an economic condition that encourages smuggling.

Market and administered smuggling are sometimes combined in illegally exporting military equipment out of a country. Thus, large quantities of arms have illegally been shipped out of the U.S. over the past decade to such countries as Cuba, Haiti, Algeria, Portugal, Israel, and Syria. Several used U.S. bombers were even included in the illegal deliveries to Portugal. One reason why these exports can be so successful is that the national border screens are primarily geared to keeping unwanted things out rather than to keeping things in. Most smuggling of goods is strictly market in character, and the receiving country is on the defensive.

Market Smuggling of Goods

Market smuggling is the operation of an international market system through the administrative screens set up in terms of limited societal interests. This smuggling is usually the result of a conflict between the *private* interests of producers, distributors, and consumers within a market and the *public* interests as expressed by legislative bodies through statute laws. The private sector in this case tends to have material ends, while the public sector tends to have social welfare, political, or military ends.

There is probably some kind of smuggling into every nation in the world today. There are, however, many "free ports" or "free zones" that have fewer screens: Hong Kong and Macao; Cayenne, French Guiana; Patagonia south of the 42nd parallel in Argentina; and the Mexican territories of Baja California and Quintana Roo and the state of Baja California. Small politically neutral countries that rely heavily on trade, such as Switzerland, have also historically served the role of intermediate trading that is sometimes useful in smuggling operations.

While particular national borders and national laws are being violated in smuggling, there are regional patterns of smuggling around the world. Tobacco and alcoholic beverages are heavily taxed in many countries, and so they flow from producing to consuming countries in many parts of the world. Cars and other luxury goods enter Argentina from the free-trade zone in southern Argentina. Cars and luxury goods (radios, record players, imported whiskeys, etc.) are smuggled into Brazil across the Uruguayan border and through the free port of Cayenne, French Guiana, to Belém on the Amazon River. Coffee is smuggled out of Brazil above the government export quota that is set to maintain coffee prices. Luxury goods flow from Japan to Korea, from West Germany and Austria to Eastern Europe, and from several sources into India. India, Pakistan, and France are the important markets for smuggled gold. Coffee is heavily taxed in West Germany, and it is smuggled in, mainly from Belgium. Swiss watches, gold, and currency are the mainstays of smugglers in Europe, cars and home appliances of Latin American smuggling. The U.S. is the most important market for gem quality diamonds and narcotics.

There are wide variations in the ability of nations to enforce their official positions on border screening due to such things as 1)the unpopularity of a law, 2) the cultural acceptance of graft in the circumvention of the law, and 3) the physical problems of detection.

The "damage" in smuggling is primarily done to the state rather than directly to individuals. Protected industries may lose some of their protection and be forced into international competition. The illegal entry of damaging substances (such as narcotics) or disease-bearing meat or produce damages society in a very general way. It is a crime that weakens the physical, social, or economic health of a society in an impersonal and indirect way. For these reasons smuggling is cross-culturally considered to be more serious by governments than by most of the members of the society. There is a consistent disparity between government and private attitudes. These systematically contrasting values are accentuated along international borders, so that international border cultures are often divided into two parts, one numerically smaller part of administrators and "policemen" who protect the general societal interest and another larger part of common people who think of smuggling in more personal terms.

Smugglers who are amateurs, small-scale operators, or simply employees of larger professional concerns are given lighter sentences and even protected by the common people, while professional smugglers are treated more harshly. Farmers along the U.S. side of the U.S.-Mexico border usually sympathize with the illegal "wetback" immigrants from Mexico and do not turn them in. The common people seem to be on the side of the *contrabandieri* who smuggle cigarettes into Italy.

x: *International Symbiosis*

Symbiosis, as a kind of cultural dynamics, is the interdependence of two or more cultural systems. Geopolitical entities—such as the states of the U.S., or nations, such as the U.S. and Mexico—develop many-stranded economic, political, and other links in a cultural network. We have the analogy from biology that specific symbiotic relationships can be *parasitic* or *mutualistic*, harmful or beneficial. However, most cultural symbiosis seems to be beneficial (mutualistic) to both systems. Warfare is the opposite of symbiosis and tends to be detrimental to both systems. Also it is more difficult to determine which is the parasite and which the damaged host in cultural relations. Americans might want to think of Mexican border cities such as Tijuana as parasitic on their nation, but there is a good historical argument for reciprocal mutualism between the U.S. and Mexico.

Just as the differing abilities that rise out of sex and age variables create a natural division and exchange of labor within the family and community, so too we find that the diverse productivity of different climates and different levels of economic development provide the basis for regional and international exchange. Pressures that oppose this exchange come from language differences, different business practices, protective immigration and import-export restrictions, and many other factors. The pressures both for and against exchange are great across the U.S.-Mexico border, but compromises are worked out so that the American and Mexican societies in the border area, while quite distinct, develop an interdependency.

America has usually been dominant in U.S.-Mexico relations. Americans originally took the land that is now the U.S. Southwest from Mexico in the Treaty of Guadalupe Hidalgo. In the early years of this century when Tijuana first boomed as a center for drinking and gambling the club owners and, of course, the clientele were predominantly Americans. The economic ties between the U.S. and Mexico are more influenced by the differential wealth of the two nations than a pattern of equal exchange of specialized products or natural resources. Mexican specialized products are primarily handmade crafts, while Mexicans buy American machine-made products. The few natural resources that Mexico exports tend to be low in cost, such as seafood.

While cultural adaptation is a two-way street in this case, with Mexican culture and society having an impact on America, the fact that America is the economically dominant partner predisposes that Mexican culture will change more than American culture and that Mexicans will generally be forced into socially subordinate roles vis-à-vis Americans. There are some advantages to the Tijuanese in this process. Highly incorporative cultures tend to be the most creative and most adaptive in their survival and growth.

The U.S. and Mexico both protect themselves from the other in terms of the flow of people, the flow of unwanted goods, and the flow of contagious diseases, but the U.S., since it is the dominant partner in the relationship and is protecting a more advanced economy, has far more stringent controls. U.S. citizens may enter Mexico as tourists freely without permits for up to 125 kilometers and for three days. With proof of U.S. citizenship it takes just a few minutes to obtain a tourist permit to travel anywhere in Mexico for six months. On the other hand, in order to enter the U.S., Mexican citizens must either obtain a Mexican passport and a U.S. visa, which takes up to about two years, or obtain a border-crossing card, which takes about one year to secure, is limited to residents of the border area, and limits travel to 25 miles for three days. In 1968 the American consulate in Tijuana denied over 33,000 immigrant applications, while issuing 8,400. It is about equally difficult for foreigners to obtain visas to work in Mexico as it is for Mexicans to obtain visas to work in the U.S. There are even a few American wetbacks who work illegally in Mexico.

Formal Cooperation

Formal cooperation to solve a problem that hurts only one of the countries has been slow to develop, in part because the two governments operate in different ways and do not interrelate very well. The Mexican government is more centralized, or vertically integrated, along national to state to municipio lines and is more dependent upon personal loyalties than legally coordinated bureaucracies. Thus, the American agencies have worked out *informal* ways to work with Mexican agencies, particularly by participating in international problem-solving associations of governors, mayors, chambers of commerce, and so forth. In these associations the public officials get together in a face-to-face social setting to talk about their problems and bargain things out. Mexican officials come away from these meetings and try to get legislative changes in Mexico that would primarily aid the Americans, while Americans campaign for changes to solve Mexican problems.

In April 1966 the Presidents of the U.S. and Mexico created the U.S.-Mexico Commission for Border Development and Friendship (CODAF) to help integrate the nine U.S. agencies and several Mexican agencies interested in the problems of the six million people who live in the vicinity of the border. However, it was abolished in 1969 by the next U.S. President's administration.

Mexico's Program Nacional Fronterizo has been building better crossing stations (as in Tijuana and Tecate) and constructed a tourist center with a museum, a hotel, and shopping facilities in Juarez on the Chamizal land. A day in April is selected each year by the U.S. and Mexico as a "Border Beautification and Friendship Day." The commission had decided to work in eleven areas as follows: 1) housing for persons of low and moderate income, 2) manpower development, 3) community centers and services, 4) libraries, 5) industrial and economic development, 6) health and sanitation, 7) transportation, 8) recreation, tourism, and beautification, 9) planning and technical assistance, 10) improved education, including vocational training, and 11) joint disaster relief. In spite of all the planning and money put into this program, improvements have been extremely slow in fruition. Improvements on the Mexican side must be done in the face of a high population increase with migrations from the interior to the border area.

There is also an annual Border Cities Conference of public officials from the cities on the two sides of the border. In January 1968 this group met in El Paso and went on record opposing U.S. Senate Bill 2790, which requires that permanent resident aliens be admitted to the U.S. only for those areas of employment which the Secretary of Labor had certified would not be adversely affected in wages and working conditions for U.S. workers. Mexican-American labor groups favor this certification requirement and tend to be in favor of constricting the flow of Mexicans into the United States to protect and improve the economic position of the Mexican-American. The International Labor Affairs Coordinating Committee meets about every month, alternately in the United States and Mexico to iron out differences. One of the committee's successful actions is directed against the use of Mexican workers in the United States as strikebreakers where a bona fide strike has been called in any industry.

The Commission of the Californias includes representatives from California, Baja California, and the Territory of

Baja California Sur. This commission has several active programs, such as the exchange of teachers and students and the control of the drug traffic. La Asociacion Cultural de Las Californias holds academic conferences each year, meeting one year in Baja California and in California the next. It has an orientation around archaelogy, history, geography, and biology, but occasionally includes a session on practical problems of concern to both Californias.

Search of the Californias, a recently organized international search and rescue group, consolidates efforts of rescue teams on both sides of the U.S.-Mexico border. The U.S. members of these teams wear a special insignia for identification to expedite their entrance into Mexico.

In 1963 Mexico lost about $28 million due to the infestation of the screwworm among cattle. The U.S. lost some cattle, too, and the screwworm was impossible to eliminate in the U.S. due to the importation of infected cattle from Mexico and the continued presence of the disease-bearing flys right across the border. The U.S. then established the Screwworm Laboratory at Mission, Texas, to produce sterile screwworm flys that are dropped in the U.S. and Mexico. About half of the fly production is dropped in each country. Additionally, the U.S. Department of Agriculture has about 30 U.S. employees and 20 Mexican employees working in Mexico on the screwworm eradication program. These efforts have eliminated the screwworm over most of the Southwest U.S. and northwest Mexico. The Mexican cattle industry has expanded so much that it now exports over 1 million cattle a year.

A rabies epidemic that became severe in 1966 in the border region was brought under control by mid-1968 through the establishment of rabies centers in Tijuana, Tecate, Mexicali, and San Luis del Rio Colorado with an initial $73,000 Mexican fund and a $97,000 grant from the U.S. Public Health Service. Between September 1966 and January 1968 5,000 stray dogs had been destroyed, and 22,000 others had been vaccinated. Then in a special two-week campaign in January 1968 that was brought on by a series of bitings by rabid dogs 8,834 dogs were vaccinated in Tijuana.

Informal Cooperation

While Mexico generally has not required prescriptions for pharmaceutical goods and has had relatively few serious internal problems about the use of drugs by Mexicans, Baja California passed a prescription law and in July 1970 made a felony of the illegal manufacture, transport, sale, or possession of barbiturates, amphetamines, and hallucinatory drugs. An earlier law already covered marijuana, cocaine, and the opiates. Both of these laws were primarily to accommodate the Americans. When formal legal coordination failed to prevent the use of one country as a sanctuary for the lawbreakers from the other country, informal liaisons between enforcement officials were successfully worked out. For example, control of the traffic in stolen cars to Mexico is often handled on an informal level. Even more informally, the Mexican residents of Jacume are allowed to crawl under the border fence to attend school, shop, and visit the post office at Jacumba, California.

Klapp and Padgett (1960) pointed out the weakness of formal political integration between San Diego and Tijuana, although this integration has increased since they wrote over a decade ago. However, there are thousands of significant kinship links between people in Tijuana and their relatives in Southern California. These are cemented by a great amount of visiting back and forth. Then there are social ties like the "Sister City" connection between Tecate and National City and similar social ties between Tijuana and Chula Vista. For example, chambers of commerce in Tijuana and Chula Vista sponsor concerts in Tijuana and an Estudiantina, a bicultural music program for students, in Chula Vista. National City and Chula Vista lie between the border and San Diego and have fairly large Mexican-American populations.

The Mexican American Neighborhood Organization (MANO) and the International Labor Affairs Coordinating Committee (with members in both San Diego and Tijuana) is helping to provide funds for a school to be built by the people of a *colonia* in the riverbed. Another volunteer school in a *colonia* east of Tijuana is being helped by an informal group in San Diego. Several orphanages receive consistent support from Americans such as Casa del Niño Pobre (Catholic), Casa de la Esperanza (Protestant), and Projecto Amigos (nondenominational). Samaritanos Voladores is a San Diego group that operates a medical clinic in Colonia Cardenas in the San Quintin Valley, 180 miles south of the border. The parent group of "Flying Samaritans" also maintains clinics in El Rosario and Colnett. The fire departments of National City and Potrero in the U.S. have been sponsoring the training of a few Mexicans each year in fire science. Tecate and Potrero actually cooperate in putting out fires in the border zone, and arrangements have been made for the fire trucks to speed through the ports of entry of both countries in case of an emergency. Mexicali cooperates with El Centro, California, and Yuma, Arizona, in running a "Border Olympics." A Tijuana vocational school has offered 100 scholarships to Spanish-speaking Americans, particularly from the San Ysidro area.

Economic Integration

Economically, Tijuana has stronger ties to the U.S. than it does to Mexico. As discussed earlier, Baja California is used as a playland by Southern Californians, a sort of additional national park for people who like to camp, fish, and swim. Tijuana itself has a 18,000-seat horse- and dog-racing stadium, two bullrings with capacities of 10,200 and 23,000, and the *jai alai* stadium which will hold a few thousand. All of these draw thousands of regular customers from Southern California.

A major factor in the growth of Tijuana and of Baja California is its proximity to Southern California, which has a population of about 14 million people and a gross product of about $50 billion—more than double that of the entire Republic of Mexico. Baja California is used by Californians as a vast park, and its interior is a favorite camping area. The Mexican government makes it easy for affluent Americans to enjoy visiting Tijuana and Baja California. Mexico allows them to enter as tourists freely for up to 125 kilometers of the border and for three days. With proof of citizenship a U.S. citizen can in a few minutes obtain a permit to travel anywhere in Mexico for six months.

A paved highway runs down the Pacific Coast for 140 miles, and then unpaved roads stretch for another 500 miles until the paved roads that run north from La Paz are reached. According to Mexico's Bureau of Tourism there is pressure from California naturalists and conversationists to keep the 500 miles unpaved to preserve Baja California as a primitive area. This conflicts with Baja California's desire to industrialize as rapidly as possible, so the government has decided to pave the highway over the next few years.

In 1933, because of the Depression and the repeal of Prohibition, Tijuana and Ensenada were declared by the Mexican government to be free perimeters with the privilege of bringing in foreign goods without duties. Later this privilege was extended to the entire peninsula. Today most foreign products that interest tourists can be imported into the area without duties and resold at rates that are lower than in the U.S. The prices and the variety of goods, combined with easy access and easy entry, lure military personnel from San Diego, affluent Los Angelenos, and industrial workers from Southern California to shop in Tijuana. The most consistent and sophisticated shoppers, however, are Mexican-Americans who are U.S. citizens. There are about 2 million Spanish surname people in California. These shoppers come south for labor intensive goods and services that are 50-60 percent cheaper in Tijuana than in San Diego.

Most of the average dollar spent by foreign visitors in

Tijuana is eventually respent by Mexicans in Southern California. Housewives cross the border to buy chickens, lard, beans, rice, eggs, potatoes, and other food items that are less expensive in the U.S. Mexican retailers and wholesalers purchase heavily in the U.S., in part simply because of the great distance to the markets of interior Mexico. More than one-half of the goods consumed in Baja California are imported, predominantly from the U.S.

One result of the interaction of the two cultures is that prostitution is one of the highest paying forms of employment for women in Tijuana. Some 300 women cater at least partially to foreign clientele. However, prostitution is being reduced by the growth of family tourism, the expansion of jobs for women, and the moral strictness of the Tijuanese.

U.S. policy has recently become stringent in regulating the flow of people and unwanted goods. In order to enter the U.S., Mexican citizens must now either obtain a Mexican passport with a U.S. visa, which takes from one day to about two years depending on the type of visa; obtain a border-crossing card, which takes about a year to secure, is limited to residents of the border area, and restricts travel to 25 miles within the U.S. for three days; or enter illegally. Despite such difficulties an average of about 35,000 Tijuanese enter the U.S. each day. Several thousand Mexican citizens reside in Tijuana where the cost of living is low and work in the U.S. where the salaries are high. These people serve as a link between U.S. and Mexican cultures, for they adapt to an industrial style of life while retaining cultural ties with Mexico. Such ties and the commerce based on them have helped to integrate northern Mexico with the U.S. Southwest.

Since these people cross from a less highly developed economy, they can also present problems to the more developed economy, when, for instance, some Mexicans become welfare cases and others undercut established wages. If the influx of workers from the less-developed economy hurts workers and unions in the more advanced economy, then the latter may act to restrict the influx. Permanent resident aliens can now be admitted to the U.S. only for those occupations which the Secretary of Labor has certified would not be adversely affected in wages and working conditions.

There is a movement in San Diego County to eliminate permanent resident aliens from the welfare rolls of San Diego County based on the fact that in order to secure a permanent resident visa most aliens were required to have an affidavit of support from a U.S. citizen sponsor. A check of the county welfare rolls revealed that 701 permanent resident aliens were receiving combined federal, state, and local relief of $397,000 a year. The district director of the U.S. Immigration and Naturalization Service said that very few of the 800,000 aliens in California had sponsors who might be held accountable for their support and he doubted that the affidavits were legally binding. In response, the State Department instructed U.S. consular officials in Mexico to be more careful in issuing visas to potential welfare recipients.

There is another dimension of economic integration which is important to Tijuana. This is Tijuana's use of used and waste goods from California. Any culture as affluent as California generates great quantities of goods that are discarded because they are too worn or damaged, out of style, or simply part of the packaging. A culture operating at a much lower economic level such as Tijuana can raise its standard of living simply by putting these discards to good use. In the 1940s San Diego's airplane industry helped to build several hundred homes in Tijuana. The packing cases of airplane engines shipped from the eastern U.S. made excellent building materials. I was surprised for a similar reason by the printing on the large cardboard box that served as siding for a house in an Indian village in Baja California, 'This is another IBM computer."

Tijuana has one of the highest per capita automobile ownership rates in Mexico, but the vast majority of those cars were purchased on the used-car lots of Southern

California. Tijuana's Chamber of Commerce lists only one new-car dealer alongside 106 used-car dealers. While Californians today make wide use of Tijuana's car-upholstery businesses, they initially developed to repair the seat covers of used cars purchased in the U.S. for sale in Tijuana.

The majority of large household appliances such as stoves and refrigerators and much of the furniture used in Tijuana are purchased on the Southern California market or are hand-me-downs from Mexican-American relatives or friends in the U.S. One of my most surprising discoveries was the extent to which second-hand houses are transported to Tijuana. The clearing out of old houses for urban renewal, for freeways, and for military projects has led to the importation of literally thousands of houses by Tijuana, especially those houses that will not meet the building codes of San Diego once they are moved. The current rate is about 400 houses a year. A house costs the movers about $300, they spend $700-$1,000 to move it, and they pay about $140 in Mexican import duties. There is a special border crossing west of the main gate in Tijuana for houses. There are also areas on both sides of the border to park houses in transit.

One of the strangest sights in Tijuana is a largely empty subdivision of about 200 houses on a hill in the La Presa area. Several years ago the subdivider purchased abandoned barracks from Miramar Air Base, moved them to La Presa, cut them into small houses, and placed them on individual sites on the hill. Only a few families moved in, in spite of the small rent of $25 a month, because the area is quite far from downtown Tijuana and because of the lack of electricity, piped water, a sewer system, and paved streets.

Life Styles and the International Border

While it is possible to show ideal types within an evolutionary classification of cities such as preindustrial-industrial-postindustrial, most cities are internally diverse in culture and transitional along this continuum. U.S. cities typically contain immigrant subcultures that are fresh from a preindustrial setting and are struggling to adapt to an industrial style. Puerto Ricans in New York, Samoans in San Francisco, and American Indians in Los Angeles are three extreme examples of this internal diversity. People with a Mexican heritage contribute heavily to the ethnic diversity in the U.S. Southwest, and while they collectively have life styles that cover the whole preindustrial-postindustrial continuum, they tend to be adapting to an industrial style of life with strong cultural ties to Mexico. These ties and the commerce based on them has helped to integrate the border zone of northern Mexico with the Southwestern U.S. This integration has also been developed through the use of northern Mexico for recreation, as a source of cheap labor, and as a source of hand-crafted goods; the use of America's cheap mass-produced goods, second-hand goods, and waste products by Mexicans; and the creative stimulus toward cultural change when cultural frontiers meet.

The cities of northern Mexico have had a rapid growth and, in some dimensions, a recent prosperity unparalleled in Mexico. Tijuana's population jumped from 21,000 in 1940 to 385,000 in 1970, with 65 percent of residents being born outside of the state of Baja California. The average daily earnings of manufacturing workers in Los Angeles County in 1968 was an estimated $27, while the equivalent figure was about $6 for Tijuana and $4 for industrial workers in Mexico generally. Clearly the great gulf in income is between the U.S. and Mexico, but Tijuana is significantly more prosperous than Mexico generally.

Northern Mexico is industrializing rapidly, but this change is taking place in the shadow of a postindustrial civilization that receives as well as gives in the relationship. The U.S. and Mexico are two dissimilar societies living together in a mutually beneficial relationship. Neither society wholly respects the other. Mexico respects the material wealth and power of the U.S., while the U.S. respects the preindustrial Mexican image of a slow, leisured life within primary communities where people are significant to each other as unique individuals.

When Americans see the industrializing and commercial border cities, they accuse these cities of not being typically Mexican. Sentiment grows with distance, and these Mexican cities are too close to the American experience to be very pleasant. America went through the same stage only a few decades earlier. The American wants to see the slow, leisured town of his image of Mexico. In fact, Americans seek out and then eventually force the commercialization of the Mexican towns that come closest to their image. Postindustrial Americans want a leisurely and artful life at an affluent level. Industrializing Mexicans want wealth and power without losing their primary communities. Both are disquieted in finding the difficulty of harmonizing their divergent values.

Many Americans are upset over their rebellious young people who espouse antimaterialism, extreme respect for individual liberty, and a social cooperation based on love rather than economic relationships. The "beat-hippie generation" is often at the forefront of the search for primary social relations within an urban society and thus idealizes Mexico, as well as American Indians, Zen Buddhists, East Indians, and other cultures that in their preindustrial stage emphasized antimaterialism, liberty, and love. To the dismay of young Americans who search out their ideal cultures, antimaterialism, liberty, and love, although often proclaimed in the world's philosophies, seem to be luxuries that are more consonant with postindustrial societies than industrializing societies. And, to the extent that they exist in preindustrial societies, antimaterialism, liberty, and love are virtually limited to those individuals who have been born and raised within the primary community. Nor has the creation of communities with these utopian ideals in urban society been particularly successful. We see the loss of liberty in communism, for example. Closer at hand, the Rancho La Puerta cooperative evolved into a commercial enterprise, and the Molokan Russian colony in Baja California seems to have failed primarily because of Mexican discrimination. The answers for the best in future social forms must lie in new social creations that are consonant with a postindustrial economy rather than the reconstruction of past societies. At any rate, urban Mexicans reject American beats and hippies, in part because Mexico is beginning to value hard work, while America is beginning to value creative leisure. The long hair of hippie men is an affront to the Mexican image of masculinity, or *machismo*. The use of drugs, while widespread in Indian Mexico hundreds of years ago, is criminal activity in modern Mexico. Finally, the hippie is dismayed to discover that urban Mexicans are probably more materialistic and have less civil rights than urban Americans.

If we become involved with people of the border culture, we find that the border is a creative stimulus of life styles, for it is never dull. We also see areas of mutual aid, reciprocity, and cooperation that are evidence that two nations at different economic levels, with differing values and languages, can achieve a working relationship which is mutually beneficial. The industrializing Mexican society acquires the wealth and knowledge of the more advanced technology and economy, while the postindustrialized U.S. society finds leisure activities, handicrafts, and a different culture to enjoy.

Bibliography

Aceves, Ricardo
    1966   *Horizontes de Baja California.* Mexico, D.F.: Central Lito-
            grafica Minera.

Anderson, Graydon K.
    1964   *The Port of Ensenada: A Report on Economic Develop-
            ment.* Economics Research Center, San Diego State Col-
            lege.

Aschmann, Homer
    1967   *The Central Desert of Baja California, Demography and
            Ecology.* Riverside, California: Manessier.

Banco de Comercio de Baja California
    1970   *Preliminary Census Report.* Mexicali.

Banco de Londres y Mexico
    1967   *Mexico in Figures.*

Banco Nacional de Mexico
    1964   *Review of the Economic Situation in Mexico* 40:461:
            8-12.

Boysen, Bernadine B.
    1970   "La Mesa Penetario: An Ethnography of Baja California's
            State Prison." Master's Thesis, San Diego State College.

Brenton, Thaddeus
    1961   *Bahia: Ensenada and Its Bay.* Los Angeles.
    1963   "Tijuana's Schools." *Baja California: Yearbook of Las
            Californias Magazine,* p. 68, San Ysidro.

Camera de Comercio de Tijuana, B.C.
    1968   *Directorio Comercial.*

Cardenas, Conrado A.
  1955   *Tijuana, Ensayo Monografico.* Mexico, D.F.: Editorial Stylo.
Chamberlin, Eugene K.
  1951   "Mexican Colonization Versus American Interests in Lower California." *The Pacific Historical Review* 20:43-45.
Christian, Chester C.
  1961   "Some Sociological Implications of Government Venereal Disease Control." Master's Thesis, University of Texas at Austin.
Community Welfare Council of Tijuana, Baja California
  1969   *Directory of Social Services, Tijuana, Baja California.*
D'Antonio, William V. and William H. Form
  1965   *Influentials in Two Border Cities: A Study in Community Decision-Making.* Notre Dame: University of Notre Dame Press.
Demaris, Ovid
  1970   *Poso del Mundo: Inside the Mexican American Border From Tijuana to Matamoros.* Boston and Toronto: Little-Brown.
Department of Industrial Relations
  1964   *Californians of Spanish Surname.* San Francisco: State of California.
Dewey, John
  1966   *The Russian Colony of Guadalupe Valley.* California State College at Los Angeles.
Dillman, C. Daniel
  1968   "Border Town Symbiosis: The Case of Brownsville and Matamoros, Twin Cities of the Lower Rio Grande." 8pp. Ms.
Dirreccion General de Estadistica
  1963   *VIII Censo General de Poblacion de Mexico, 1960, Estado de Baja California.*
  1963   *Compendio Estadisco, 1962.*
  1965A *La Poblacion Economicamente Activa de Mexico en Junio, 1964.*
  1965B *Revista de Estadistica* 28.
  1966   *Revista de Estadistica* 29.
Freithaler, William
  1968   "The Economic Development of the United States-Mexico Border Region." 12pp. Ms.

Gerhard, Peter and Howard E. Gulick
  1967   *Lower California: A Descriptive Traveler's Guide.* Glendale, Calif.: Arthur H. Clark.
Klapp, Orrin E. and L. Vincent Padgett
  1960   "Power Structure and Decision-Making in a Mexican Border City." *American Journal of Sociology* 65:400-406.
Lingenfelter, Richard E.
  1967   *The Rush of '89.* Los Angeles: Dawson's.
Little, Arthur D. (de Mexico)
  1966   *Manufacturing in Mexico for the U.S. Market.* Mexico, D.F.
MacNamara, Patrick H.
  1971   "Prostitution Along the U.S.-Mexican Border: A Survey." *Border-State University Consortium for Latin America, Occasional Papers* 2:1-21. University of Texas at El Paso.
Martinez, Pablo L.
  1960   *History of Lower California.* Mexico, D.F.: Editorial Sobre Baja California.
Nordhoff, Charles
  1888   *Peninsular California.* New York: Harper & Bros. Appendix 2.
Price, John A.
  1967   Editor. *Tecate: An Industrial Town on the Mexican Border.* U.C.L.A. Ethnographic Field School Report, Los Angeles.
  1968A Editor. *Tijuana '68: Ethnographic Notes on a Mexican Border City.* San Diego, California.
  1968B "Tijuana: A Study of Symbiosis." *New Mexico Quarterly* 38:3:8-18.
  1971A "Baja California in Anthropological Theory: Desert Adaptation, Cul-de-Sac, Frontier, and Border." *Pacific Coast Archaeological Society Quarterly* 7:1:27-33.
  1971B "International Border Screens and Smuggling." *Border-State University Consortium for Latin America, Occasional Papers* 2:22-42.
Price, John A. and Helen C. Smith
  1971   "A Bibliography on the Anthropology of Baja California." *Pacific Coast Archaeological Society Quarterly* 7:1:39-69.
Programa National Fronterizo
  1961   Mexico, D.F.

Ridgely, Roberta
1966-68 "The Man Who Built Tijuana." *San Diego.*

Rubel, Arthur J.
1966 *Across the Tracks: Mexican-Americans in a Texas City.* Austin, Texas: University of Texas Press.

Ruddle, Kenneth and Mukhtar Hamour, eds.
1972 *Statistical Abstract of Latin America 1970.* Los Angeles: Latin America Center, U.C.L.A.

Samora, Julian
1966 Editor. *La Raza: Forgotten Americans.* Notre Dame: University of Notre Dame Press.
1971 *Los Mojados: The Wetback Story.* Notre Dame: University of Notre Dame Press.

Schmieder, Oscar
1928 "Lower California Studies: The Russian Colony of Guadalupe Valley." *University of California Publications in Geography* 2:14:409-434.

Secretaria de Industria y Comercio
1967 *Anuario Estadistico de los Estados Unidos Mexicanos: 1964-1965,* Mexico, D.F.

Seitz, Robert J.
1970 "Frontier Beat." *I and N Reporter,* January, pp. 34-41. Immigration and Naturalization Service, Washington, D.C.

Stoddard, Ellwyn R.
1970 "Comparative Structures and Attitudes along the U.S.-Mexico Border." *Border-State University Consortium for Latin America, Occasional Papers.* University of Texas at El Paso.

Texas A. & M. University
1966 *Occupational Change Among Spanish Americans.* College Station, Texas.

Tichbone, Roger
1970, "Tales of Mexico and Marijuana." *Scanlan's* 1:6:7-20.

United Nations
1972 *Demographic Yearbook: 1971.* New York.

U.S. Bureau of Census
1972 *Statistical Abstract of the United States: 1972.* Washington, D.C.

U.S. Immigration and Naturalization Service
1968 *Annual Report.* Washington, D.C.

Valencia, Nester A.
   1968   "Urbanization in the Ciudad Juarez-El Paso Region." 14
          pp. Ms.
Whetten, Nathan L.
   1968   "Population Growth in Mexico." *Report of the U.S. Se-
          lect Commission on Western Hemisphere Immigration*, pp.
          173-184. Washington, D.C.
Winnie, William
   1960   "Estimates of Interstate Migration in Mexico, 1950-1960,
          Data and Methods." *Anthropologica* 14.
Zahn, Curtis
   1944   "The Orphan Nobody Wants." *Westways* 16:4:14-15.

Index

San Ysidro, 14, 19, 45, 62, 112, 149
Screening, 43, 59, 60, 163-169
Sewer facilities, 76-80, 135
Smuggling, 169-172
    drugs, 99-116
    laws, 106-109
Squatters, 20, 27, 34-35, 76
Symbiosis, 15, 42, 146-148, 155, 160, 173-186

T
Tecate, 24, 129-148, 176-178

Tourism, 9-10, 28, 32, 36, 49, 61, 88-92, 113, 147, 180
    military, 59, 93
Treaty of Guadalupe Hidalgo, 30, 45-46

U
Urban problems, 20, 25, 27, 78, 139
Used goods, 182-183

W
Water, 76-80, 135